How to Train Your
Dachshund

liz palika

DACHSHUND

Photos by the author unless
otherwise credited.

The Publisher would like to thank the owners of all the dogs in this book, including Ellane Baum, Penni Cronk, Robin Gianopoulos, Lucy Granowicz, Maureen Greer, Harvey and Judy Kratzer, Kaye Ladd, Pat Leone, Cathy Marzluf, Bonnie Mercier, Diane Poranski, Barbara Starnes, Wendy Tillotson, and Gwen Wexler.

© T.F.H. Publications, Inc.

Distributed in the UNITED STATES to the Pet Trade by T.F.H. Publications, Inc., 1 TFH Plaza, Neptune City, NJ 07753; on the Internet at www.tfh.com; in CANADA by Rolf C. Hagen Inc., 3225 Sartelon St., Montreal, Quebec H4R 1E8; Pet Trade by H & L Pet Supplies Inc., 27 Kingston Crescent, Kitchener, Ontario N2B 2T6; in ENGLAND by T.F.H. Publications, PO Box 74, Havant PO9 5TT; in AUSTRALIA AND THE SOUTH PACIFIC by T.F.H. (Australia), Pty. Ltd., Box 149, Brookvale 2100 N.S.W., Australia; in NEW ZEALAND by Brooklands Aquarium Ltd., 5 McGiven Drive, New Plymouth, RD1 New Zealand; in SOUTH AFRICA by Rolf C. Hagen S.A. (PTY.) LTD., P.O. Box 201199, Durban North 4016, South Africa; in JAPAN by T.F.H. Publications. Published by T.F.H. Publications, Inc.

MANUFACTURED IN THE
UNITED STATES OF AMERICA
BY T.F.H. PUBLICATIONS, INC.

contents

INTRODUCTION

As a dog obedience class instructor, I see a variety of breeds come through my classes. As breeds gain or lose popularity, I may see more or less of them. However, some remain relatively stable in number, and Dachshunds are one of those breeds. I usually have at least one Dachshund in any given puppy or basic obedience class.

Generally, Dachshunds do well in training, but once in a while I see a situation in which both the dog and owner are unhappy, and I can tell it's only going to get worse. This is often the result of the owner not understanding what kind of pet a Dachshund would be before acquiring one.

I have had Doxie owners come to class expecting their dog to behave like their previous pet, perhaps a Golden Retriever or German Shepherd. It's not going to happen! Doxies are not like other breeds and never will be. They can be fierce watchdogs and can be surprisingly aggressive. Doxies are playful, excitable, domineering, and on a bad day, can be quite destructive. On the other hand, they are very affectionate with their owners.

It's important that potential Doxie owners understand what a Dachshund is by nature before bringing one home. This is a very nice breed of dog but is certainly not for everyone. Dachshund owners also need to know how to train their dog so that he can fit into their lives as smoothly and quietly as possible.

In this book I have tried to present Dachshund owners (and prospective Dachshund owners) with realistic options abut choosing a Dachshund for them and good information about training that dog. Dachshunds can be a wonderful family pet and companion as well as a super hunting dog. With help from their owner, Dachshunds can be a friend, a partner, and a great companion.

Before you bring a Dachshund home, make sure that this is the right breed for you. Doxies, by nature, are playful, excitable, and affectionate; however, they need a strong and firm owner.

dachshund

SELECTING
the Right Dog for You

WHAT ARE DACHSHUNDS?

Dogs have been used for hunting for hundreds of years. Scent hounds, for example, have hunted game for the table or fire spit for as long as dogs have been domesticated. A variety of breeds were developed to control pests or dangerous animals. The larger (30 – 35 pound), short-legged Dachshund was developed in Germany centuries ago to hunt badgers. Badgers were a threat to farmers' livestock, and packs of these short-legged, tenacious, stubborn Dachshunds were sent down badger holes after them. In the same manner, the medium-sized Dachshund (16 – 24 pounds) was used to hunt small predators, including foxes, while the smallest-sized Dachshund (10 pounds or less) was used to flush weasels or rabbits from their holes.

Developed in Germany centuries ago, the larger, short-legged Dachshund was used to hunt badgers, while the medium-sized Doxie was used to hunt small predators. The smallest-sized Doxie flushed weasels and rabbits from their holes.

dachshund

Photo by Isabelle Francais

Most people are attracted to Doxies because of their small size, attractive coat, and playful nature. However, Doxies are known to be occasionally stubborn and resistant to training.

d a c h s h u n d

The Dachshund came to the United States over a hundred years ago and was recognized by the American Kennel Club (AKC) in 1885. To maintain the breed's tenacity and hunting expertise, field trials were instituted in 1935. The US Dachshund Field Trial Club held its first field trial, wherein Doxies were put to ground in artificial rabbit burrows and judged by the German rules for field trials.

In 1935, the newly formed Dachshund Club of America held its first field trial in Lamington, NJ, under rules written for American competition. Titles were offered for competition, with the best dogs competing for the coveted Field Trial Champion title.

The Dachshund Today

The Dachshund of today comes in a number of varieties. There are three coat types: longhaired, wirehaired, and smooth. In addition, there are two sizes allowed: the miniature, weighing less than 11 pounds when over a year of age; and the standard, weighing more than 11 pounds when over a year of age. This means that there are essentially six

The Dachshund of today has a variety of coat types: longhaired, wirehaired, and smooth, which range in color from red to gray to white with patches or spots. These adorable puppies are an example of smooth-haired standard Dachshunds.

different types of Dachshund: smooth miniatures, smooth standards, longhaired miniatures, longhaired standards, wirehaired miniatures, and wirehaired standards.

There are also color variations. The most widely recognized color is a dark reddish brown, called "red." But Doxies may also be black, chocolate, gray, or even white; each of these colors will have copper markings above the eyes, on the cheeks, inner ears, inside the legs, and under the tail. Doxies may also be dappled. These dogs are light brown or gray, sometimes even white, with darker, irregularly shaped patches or spots throughout the coat.

The Dachshund's body shape is well known, with short legs and a long, slender body. The body is in proportion, whether the dog is a standard or a miniature. Although some Doxies do get heavy, the breed description calls for a compact figure (not a heavy one), and the dog should be athletic enough to hunt.

Temperament

Because of their appearance, Dachshunds attract a number of people. The Miniature's small

DACHSHUNDS IN ART
The Dachshund, with his unique build, has been well represented in art throughout the years. One of the most famous of these paintings is part of the American Kennel Club's collection. A Dachshund, named Judy, is portrayed standing with her front feet on a rabbit. The painter, George Earl, is well known for his canine art.

size, different coat types, and appealing long body, coupled with the breed's playfulness and high activity level, suits a variety of tastes. Although many are drawn to the breed, Dachshunds have characteristics that can make them less than desirable pets for some people.

One feature of the Doxie personality that is considered undesirable is the breed's stubbornness. Dachshund owners will readily admit that their dogs are obstinate, a familiar breed trait. However, there was once a reason that this particular personality quirk was necessary. Badgers are tough characters and ferocious, tenacious predators. Therefore, the Dachshund sent to drive badgers from their den had to be just as tough and tenacious as the animal he was hunting or he couldn't get the job done. Even though very few Doxies actually hunt badgers in present day, that personality trait remains.

Benjamin L. Hart, DVM, and Lynette A. Hart, authors of *The Perfect Puppy*, state that Dachshunds rank in the lowest percentiles for ease of obedience training and housetraining. In other words, compared to many other popular breeds, Dachshunds do not always accept training well. This does not mean that Dachshunds are untrainable; far from it. But it does suggest that the owners of a Dachshund must know how to motivate him to want to be good so that life is not a constant battle.

The Harts continued by saying, "Dachshunds rank high in territorial defense; these are believable watchdogs. Doxies may also be aggressive toward other dogs, not a positive trait, and they have been known to be snippy toward children. These traits must be carefully considered before adding a Doxie to the family."

A Dachshund left alone in the backyard all day is a lonely dog. Isolated and away from his pack, he will bark and howl. However, two Dachshunds could do quite well together.

Photo by Isabelle Francais

Although Doxies are affectionate dogs, they are not the best choice if you want a dog that will remain by your side. Like most dogs, Doxies do need to spend time with their people.

Usually not a cuddly dog, a Dachshund is not the best choice if you are looking for a dog that will snuggle at your feet and follow you from room to room. Although Dachshunds do need to spend time with their owners, especially as puppies so that they can bond well with their people, they will never be snugglers like many other breeds.

IS A DACHSHUND THE RIGHT BREED FOR YOU?

Evaluating Your Personality and Lifestyle

Adding a dog to your family is like adopting a new family member. This is a 14-year obligation that should not be taken lightly. Take some time to think about this commitment prior to making a final decision.

Do you work long hours and come home tired? When you come home, would you rather relax than do anything else? If so, you should probably adopt a pair of older Dachshunds. The two could keep each other company when you aren't at home, and older dogs would be less energetic and less demanding of you.

Do you come home tired, but enjoy doing things outdoors when you're at home? Two younger adult Dachshunds might suit your lifestyle. Again, they could keep each other company while you're at work, but younger dogs would be willing to go places and do things with you when you have free time.

Do you have a flexible schedule, work short hours, or spend a lot of time at home? In these situations, a puppy might be the right choice for you.

Some people get a dog so that they can be the center of someone's world; they love the companionship and the devotion that many dogs show their owners. If you want a dog that follows you from room to room, and always lies at your feet and wants to be close to you, don't get a Dachshund. A Dachshund will know where you are, in what room and how far away, but doesn't necessarily need to follow you there. Of course, if you go to

If you prefer a Doxie puppy to an older dog, it's important that your schedule allows for the time needed to raise an energetic and untrained puppy.

Photo by Isabelle Francais

the kitchen, your Dachshund will suddenly be underfoot— but there's some added motivation to be there!

The Dachshund's Needs

All dogs have some specific needs, so before you get a Dachshund, think about these requirements. It could make the difference between a successful relationship with your dog or the need to give him up later.

First, remember that Dachshunds are pack dogs; they were bred to hunt with other Dachshunds. A Dachshund is not a good dog to leave alone.

If you love the breed and really want to own a Dachshund but cannot spend most of the day with your dog, you should consider having two.

You must be willing to spend time exercising your Dachshund. These are active dogs originally bred to hunt rabbits, badgers, and other predators. Although they may not seem to fit our idea of an athlete, Doxies are energetic dogs that need daily vigorous exercise.

Your Dachshund will also need a good training program. He'll need to learn social and

Because Doxies are pack dogs that were bred to hunt with each other, they do not prefer to be alone. If you cannot spend most of the day with your Dachshund, then you should consider getting two dogs, or in this case, a whole bunch!

Photo by Isabelle Francais

dachshund

household rules, and you'll need to be able to control his barking so that you don't get any complaints from your neighbors. In addition, you'll need to be able to train him so you can limit his destructive tendencies.

Your Dachshund should have a securely fenced yard or dog run. Being a hunting dog, a Dachshund follows his nose and doesn't always think about where his nose is leading him—out of the yard, down the block, across the busy street, or far, far away. Dachshunds need a secured area to protect them from themselves.

SELECTING THE RIGHT DOG

Male or Female?

There are a lot of myths concerning the traits of males and females. Ultimately, every dog has an individual personality regardless of gender. Spayed bitches (females) and neutered dogs (males) are usually a little calmer than those that are not. Spaying and neutering removes sexual hormones and as a result, the sexual tension that can accompany those hormones. To be a good pet and companion, your dog doesn't need those

> **A DOG RUN**
> A fenced-in area that is 6 feet wide by 20 feet long is adequate for two Dachshunds. Bigger is better, of course, but a dog run this size is just fine. The run should be secure, covered (if possible), and offer protection from the sun and weather.

hormones anyway.

Male Dachshunds do tend to be a little bigger than females

Although male Dachshunds do tend to be slightly larger than females, there aren't many other differences between the two sexes. Dogs that are spayed or neutered are usually calmer than those that are not. Here, Greg Berg and "Calla" enjoy an afternoon in the sun.

and slightly heavier boned. Because the Dachshund is not a large dog anyway, this doesn't make much difference. The male will mark his territory by lifting his leg and urinating, which can be an annoying habit. Neutered males tend to do it less, and training can help control this instinct.

What Age?

All puppies are adorable, including Dachshund puppies. However, they are a lot of work. Puppies eat, sleep, relieve themselves, play, and then start the whole cycle all over again.

When you add a puppy to the family, you should expect at least two years of puppyhood before your Dachshund is grown up, mentally as well as physically. When your Dachshund puppy is full grown, you will have a wonderful friend and companion, but it will require about two years of your time and effort to get to that point.

If you aren't sure you have the time, patience, and energy to raise a puppy, think about getting an adult dog instead. Many adult Dachshunds need new homes—perhaps an owner

Although they are cute, puppies are a bundle of energy that require a lot of time, work, and patience. If you can't provide those things, you might want to consider adopting an older Dachshund.

Photo by Isabelle Francais

passed away or was transferred overseas—and these dogs can make very good pets.

Just as with raising a puppy, there are some negative factors to think about before adopting an adult dog. Adopting an adult dog can be compared to buying a used car—sometimes you get a gem; sometimes you get a lemon. You don't always know how the dog was treated prior to his adoption. Often, the dog's past treatment, training (or lack thereof), and even health care could affect his future behavior.

You must also be willing to be patient with the dog while he settles into your household. It takes newly adopted dogs at least three months to settle down. Until the dog realizes that he's there for good, you won't see his true personality and behavior.

Finding an Adult Dog

If you have decided that an adult dog would be a better choice for you than a puppy, there are a few places you can look for a new companion. Check with your local humane society or animal shelter. Many people who give up their dogs for whatever reason often leave them at a shelter. You can also check the classified

RESCUE GROUPS

Most breed clubs sponsor or run breed rescue groups. These groups screen the dogs taken in for adoption as to their personality, temperament, and training (or lack of training). This prescreening can be beneficial to you, because it will give you a head start when deciding whether or not a particular dog might be the right one for you. Dogs handled by rescue groups are also vaccinated, spayed or neutered, and examined for other health problems. Your local shelter can give you the phone number of a Dachshund rescue group near you.

advertisements in your local newspaper or the bulletin board at the veterinarian's office.

Evaluating an Adult Dog

Once you have found an adult Dachshund, how do you decide whether or not this dog is right for you? First of all, do you like the dog? Your feelings for the animal are certainly going to play a big part in any future relationship. If you don't like the dog now, don't expect that to change later.

Do you know why this dog was given up by his owner? Dogs can be given up for many reasons. Sometimes a dog is

Photo by Isabelle Francais

If you decide to adopt an older Dachshund, make sure that your personalities are compatible. Hopefully, the Doxie that you choose is housetrained and has had previous obedience training.

dachshund

given up through no fault of his own. However, if he was given up because of behavior problems, you need to know that. Perhaps the dog barked too much and the neighbors complained. Maybe he wasn't housetrained or hasn't had any obedience training; these are important issues.

What is the dog's personality like? When you whistle, does the dog cock his head to the side and look at you? Does he come over to visit with you? If he comes up to you wagging his tail, great! However, if he looks sideways at you, slinks, or bares his throat, be careful. This Dachshund is worried, fearful, or shy and could potentially be a problem. If the dog stands on his tiptoes and stares at you, leave him alone. He's challenging you and could be potentially aggressive—and even a dog only 11 inches tall could be dangerous.

Ideally, you want a dog that is happy to see you without showing too much worry or fearfulness and without showing any aggression. You want a dog that is housetrained and hopefully has had some obedience training. Make sure his behavior problems are ones that you can live with for the time being, until you have an opportunity to train him.

Finding a Puppy

If you have the time and patience to raise a puppy, wonderful! You will want to find a reputable breeder to buy a puppy from, so that you can get the best puppy possible. Breeder referrals can come from many places. Perhaps a neighbor has a nice Dachshund; ask her where she got her dog. Your veterinarian might have a client whose Dachshund produces healthy puppies. You may also want to attend a dog show in your area to talk to other owners and handlers of the breed.

Once you find a few breeders, make appointments to talk with them and ask a few questions. "Are you active in shows or dog sports?" A breeder who shows her Dachshunds in conformation shows will raise dogs that are good representatives of the breed. If she competes in obedience trials, her dogs are trainable. However, if she runs her Dachshunds in a hunting brace, they may not be the best choice for you if you're looking for a suburban pet.

"Do you belong to the

national or regional Dachshund clubs?" Most clubs publish newsletters or magazines that usually contain articles concerning the breed's health and well-being.

"What health problems have you seen in your breed?" Dachshunds are healthy dogs, but a line with no problems whatsoever is unusual. The breeder should be honest with you about potential health threats and what she's doing to prevent them.

"Can you provide me with a list of references?" She will, of course, give you references to people who are happy with her dogs, but that's okay, too. You can still ask them questions. Did the breeder follow through with everything she agreed to supply, including the puppy's paperwork? Would you buy another puppy from her?

A caring breeder will ask you as many questions as you asked her. She will want to make sure you are the right person for her puppy. Don't get defensive about her questions; instead, answer them truthfully. If by some chance she says her dogs are

Evaluate your prospective puppy's temperament by taking him away from his mother and littermates. An extroverted puppy will come to you eagerly and try to climb into your lap.

Photo by Isabelle Francais

dachshund

not right for you, listen to her. She knows her dogs better than you do, and she's probably right.

Evaluating a Puppy

Each puppy has his or her own personality—just as you have yours—and finding the right personality to match yours can sometimes be a challenge. If you are outgoing, extroverted, and active, a quiet, withdrawn, shy puppy would not fit well into your household. That puppy would do better in the household of a person who is just as quiet as he is.

When you look at a litter of puppies, a few simple tests can help you to evaluate each puppy's temperament. Take one puppy away from his mother and littermates. Place him on the ground and walk a few steps away. Squat down and call him to you. An outgoing, extroverted puppy will come to you and try to climb into your lap. If you stand up and walk away, the extrovert will follow you, trying to get underfoot. If you throw a piece of crumpled paper a few feet away, he will go after the paper, shake it, and try to shred it. This puppy will do well with someone who is just as much an extrovert as he

> ### BE CAREFUL
> On average, Dachshunds live 14 years. Adding a Dachshund to your family is a long-term commitment, so make sure getting a dog is the right decision for you. Think it through very carefully and only bring a dog home when you know he will fit in well with your lifestyle and schedule.

is. He will need lots of exercise, good training, and a job to occupy his mind.

The quiet, submissive puppy will come to you when you call, but may do a belly crawl or roll over to bare his belly. When you walk away, he may follow you or he may watch you but be hesitant to follow. When you throw the paper, he may go after it but hesitate to bring it back. This puppy will need a quiet owner, positive training, and gentle handling.

These two puppies are extremes for Dachshund temperaments; most are somewhere in between these two examples. Try to find a puppy with a personality more like your own. Do not get a quiet puppy and hope that you can liven him up. Nor should you get the extroverted puppy and think that you can calm him down. It won't work. Instead, get the puppy that is right for you.

Canine
DEVELOPMENT
Stages

IN THE BEGINNING

Hunting dogs, including Dachshunds, have a long history of working and living with mankind. In spite of this long, shared history, the bond that we have with dogs must be renewed with each puppy; the bond itself is not hereditary, although the tendency to bond is. This relationship is what makes owning a dog so special. To understand when and how this bond develops, it's important to understand that your Dachshund is a dog, not a person in a fuzzy dog suit.

FAMILIES AND PACKS

Most researchers agree that the ancestors of today's dogs were wolves. They disagree on which wolves those ancestors were—either today's gray wolves or perhaps a species of wolf that is now extinct. In any event, wolves are social creatures that live in an

Because dogs are pack animals, experts feel that they adapt well to the human family. The family as a whole is very important to a Doxie. The term "one-person dog" rarely ever applies to a Dachshund.

Photo by Isabelle Francais

extended family pack. The pack might consist of a dominant (alpha) male and a dominant (alpha) female, and they are usually the only two that breed. It will also include subordinate males and females, juveniles, and puppies. A very harmonious group, wolves hunt and play together, defend their territory against intruders, and care for each other. Discord only occurs when there is a change in the pack order. If one of the leaders becomes disabled, if an adult leaves the pack, or if a subordinate adult tries to assume dominance, there may be some jockeying around to fill the dominant position.

Many experts feel that domesticated dogs adapt very well to our lifestyle because we, too, live in groups. Although we call our groups families instead of packs, they are nevertheless social groups. However, the comparison isn't quite accurate; our families are much more chaotic than the average wolf pack! We are terribly inconsistent with our social norms and rules for behavior. (For example, we let our Dachshund jump up and paw us when we're in grubby clothes and yell at him when he jumps up on our good clothes!) To the dog, our communication

skills are also confusing; our voice says one thing, while our body language says something else. To our dogs, we are very complex, confusing creatures. So, yes, we can say that both dogs and humans live in social groups, and we can use that comparison to understand a little more about our dogs. However, we must also understand that our families are very different from a wolf pack.

Because Dachshunds are very much a pack dog—Doxies traditionally hunted in a brace (two dogs) or in a pack (more than two dogs)—the pack is very important to them. To a Dachshund, the family as a whole is much more important than one person. You've heard of the term a "one-person dog?" That rarely, if ever, applies to a Dachshund.

FROM BIRTH TO FOUR WEEKS OF AGE

For the first three weeks of life, the family and the pack are unimportant as far as the baby Dachshund is concerned. The only one of any significance to him is his mother. She is the key to his survival and the source of food, warmth, and security.

At four weeks of age, the baby Dachshund's needs are still being met by his mother,

Photo by Vince Serbin

A newborn Dachshund depends on his mother for most of his basic needs, but his littermates do provide warmth and security when the mother is absent.

instinctive training will be vitally important to the puppies' future acceptance of discipline and training.

The breeder should be socializing the puppies now and getting them used to being handled by people. At this age, they can learn the difference between their mother's touch and gentle handling by humans.

WEEKS FIVE THROUGH SEVEN

The young Dachshund goes through some tremendous changes between five and seven weeks of age. He is learning to but his littermates are becoming more important. His brothers and sisters provide warmth and security when their mother leaves the nest. His curiosity is developing, and he will climb on and over his littermates, learning their scent and feel. During this period, he will begin to use his sense of hearing to follow sounds and his sense of vision to follow moving objects.

Mom will also begin disciplining the puppies—very gently, of course—and this

---

LET THE MOTHER DOG CORRECT

Some inexperienced breeders will stop the mother dog from correcting her puppies, perhaps thinking that she is impatient, tired, or a poor mother. When the mother dog is not allowed to correct the puppies naturally, they do not learn how to accept discipline and therefore, have a hard time later on when their new owner tries to establish some rules. Orphaned puppies raised by people suffer from the same problems. A mother dog knows instinctively what to do for her babies and sometimes a correction—a low growl, a bark, or a snap of the teeth—is exactly what is needed.

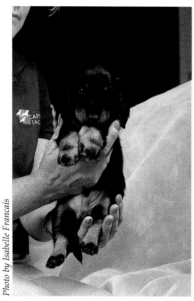

A puppy goes through many stages of development. At five to seven weeks of age, a puppy is learning how to recognize people and is responding to individual voices.

recognize people and is starting to respond to individual voices. Playing, wrestling, and scuffling more with his littermates will teach the puppy how to get along, how to play, when the play is too rough, when to be submissive, and when to take things seriously. His mother's discipline at this stage of development teaches the puppy to accept corrections, training, and affection.

Puppies should never be taken from their mother at this stage of development. Puppies taken away too early and sent to new homes may have lasting behavior problems. They often have difficulty dealing with other dogs, may have trouble accepting rules and discipline, and may become excessively shy, aggressive, or fearful.

THE EIGHTH WEEK

The eighth week of life is a frightening time for most puppies. Puppies will go through several fear periods as they grow up, and this is the first one. Even though this is the traditional time that most puppies go to their new homes, they would actually benefit by staying with their littermates for one more week. If a puppy leaves the breeder's home during this fear period and is frightened by the car ride home, he may retain that fear of car rides for the rest of his life. In fact, this stress is why so many puppies do get carsick!

This also applies to the puppy's new home, his first trip to the veterinarian's office, or anything else that frightens him.

WEEKS NINE THROUGH TWELVE

The baby Dachshund can go to his new home anytime during the ninth and tenth weeks of life. At this age, he is ready to

Photo by Isabelle Francais

At 12 weeks of age, a puppy is ready to go to his new home. Begin socializing him at this time and make sure that he has had all of his necessary vaccinations.

your baby Dachshund is not frightened by these things as you introduce them. For example, once your puppy has had some vaccinations (check with your veterinarian), take him with you to the pet store when you go to buy dog food. While there, introduce him to the store clerks, other customers, and even to the store parrot. Your trip there could also include walking up some stairs, walking on slippery floors, and going through an automatic door. All of these things, introduced gradually and with encouragement, and repeated in various environments, add up to a confident, well-socialized puppy.

form permanent relationships. Take advantage of this and spend time with your puppy, playing with him and encouraging him to explore his new world. Teach him his name by calling him in a happy, high-pitched tone of voice. Encourage him to follow you by backing away from him, patting your leg, and calling him to you.

Socialization is very important now, too. It is more than simply introducing your puppy to other people, dogs, noises, and sounds. Socialization is making sure

During this stage of development, your Dachshund puppy's pack instincts are developing. He is beginning to understand which people belong to his pack or family and which don't. Do not let him growl at visitors during this stage; he is much too young to understand when and how to protect. Instead, stop the growling and let him know that you, as his pack leader, can protect the family.

You can show him his position in the family in several ways, but one of the easiest is

Photo by Isabelle Francais

A gentle tummy rub is an easy way to show your Doxie that you are the boss. By baring his belly to you, he is assuming a submissive position.

to lay him down, roll him over, and give him a tummy rub. This exercise may seem very simple, but by baring his tummy, he is assuming a submissive position to you. When his mother corrected him by growling or barking at him, he would roll over and bare his tummy to her, in essence telling her, "Okay! I understand, you're the boss!" When you have him roll over for a tummy rub, you are giving him the same message, but you are doing it in a very gentle, loving way.

During this stage of development, love, affection, and security are important as well, but right now your

As they grow, puppies will try to establish their position in the family pack. Make sure that you and everyone in the family are consistent in enforcing household rules.

RETRIEVING

Begin retrieving games at 9 to 12 weeks of age. Get your Dachshund's attention with a toy he likes and then toss it four to six feet away. When he grabs the toy, call him back to you in a happy tone of voice. Praise him enthusiastically when he brings it back to you. If he runs away and tries to get you to chase him, stand up and walk away, stopping the game completely. Don't chase him! Let him learn now, while he's young, that he must play by your rules. Chasing a ball or soft flying disk can be great exercise for a puppy and can teach him to accept discipline, which will set the stage for a sound working relationship later.

Dachshund puppy needs to learn that his life is governed by some rules. Don't allow him to do anything now that you won't want him to continue doing later as a full-grown adult.

WEEKS THIRTEEN THROUGH SIXTEEN

From 13 through 16 weeks of age, your Dachshund puppy will be trying to establish his position in your family pack. If you were able to set some rules during earlier stages of development, this period won't be quite so difficult. However, if you caved in to that adorable Dachshund puppy face, well, this could be a challenging time.

Consistency in enforcing household rules is very important now, and everyone in the family or household should be enforcing rules in the same way. Dachshunds are very perceptive, and if your puppy senses a weak link in the chain of command, he will take advantage of it. This doesn't mean he's a bad puppy—it simply means he's a smart puppy.

Puppies with dominant personalities may start mounting behavior toward small children in the family or toward his toys. Obviously, this is undesirable behavior and should be stopped immediately—just don't let it happen.

Socialization with people, friendly dogs, and other such experiences should continue throughout this stage of development.

WEEKS SEVENTEEN THROUGH TWENTY SIX

Sometime between 17 and 26 weeks of age, most puppies go through another fear period much like the one they went through at 8 weeks of age. Things that the puppy had previously accepted as normal may suddenly become frightening. A friend's Dachshund walked into the

As they grow, puppies will try to establish their position in the family pack. Make sure that you and everyone in the family are consistent in enforcing household rules.

dachshund

Photo by Isabelle Francais

Even though Dachshunds are naturally protective dogs, do not encourage your Doxie to be overly aggressive.

backyard and began barking fearfully at a picnic table that had been in the same spot prior to the puppy joining the family. It was as if he had never noticed the table before and all at once found it very scary!

Make sure you don't reinforce any of these fears. If you pet or cuddle your puppy or tell him softly, "It's okay, sweetie, don't be afraid," he will hear the soft words and feel the petting and assume that these are positive reinforcements for his fears. In other words, your puppy will think he was right to be afraid. Instead, walk up to

whatever is scaring him and touch it—letting him see you touch it—as you tell him, "Look at this!" in a happy tone of voice. Use a fun, playful tone so that he can see that the thing he is afraid of really isn't scary at all.

Your Dachshund's protective instincts will continue to develop throughout this stage. If he continues to show protectiveness or aggression (by growling, snarling, barking, or raising his hackles), interrupt his behavior by turning him away or distracting him. If you encourage this behavior too early or if you correct it too harshly, you will overemphasize it and your puppy may continue to do it. Too much emphasis at this young age may result in overprotectiveness or fearfulness in your dog as he grows up. Instead, react calmly and just stop it from happening.

Dachshunds are naturally protective as adults and if you wanted a Dachshund for this trait, don't worry about interrupting the behavior now. Training will not hamper those instincts. At this age, your Dachshund puppy doesn't know what or when to protect. Instead of letting him take over and learn bad habits, stop his behavior and let him know you are in charge. Later, when he's more mature, you can encourage the specific protectiveness you want.

THE TEENAGE MONTHS

The teenage months in a dog's life are very much like the teenage years in a human child's life. Human adolescents in their teens are feeling strong and are striving to prove their ability to take care of themselves. They

It's normal for your Doxie to show disobedience during his adolescence, especially in the teenage months. Be consistent and let him know that you are the leader.

Photo by Isabelle Francais

Photo by Isabelle Francais

The teenage months are a critical time for a puppy. Make sure that you act like his leader and not his best friend, which could cause a dominant personality to regard you as weak.

dachshund

want to be independent, yet they still want the security of home. These two conflicting needs seem to drive some teens (and their parents) absolutely crazy.

Dogs can be very much the same way. Dachshunds in adolescence push the boundaries of their rules, trying to see if you really will enforce them. Most Dachshund owners say that their dogs act "too full of themselves"during this stage of growing up.

In Dachshunds, the teenage stage usually hits at about 12 months of age, although it's not unusual to see it happen a month or two earlier. You'll know when it has occurred. One day you will ask your previously well-trained dog to do something he knows very well, such as sit, and he'll look at you as if you're nuts. He's never heard that word before in his life and even if he had, he still wouldn't do it!

Another common behavior would be a regression in social skills. Your previously well-socialized Dachshund may start barking at other dogs or jumping on people. He may start getting rough with children or may start chasing the cat.

Dachshunds are considered mature at two years of age. They may experience one more fear period, but it's usually the last.

During this stage of development, you really need to consistently enforce social and household rules. Hopefully, you will have already started obedience training because that control will help. If you haven't started obedience training, do so now—don't wait any longer.

Make sure, too, that your dog regards you as the leader. This is not the time to try to be best friends—that would cause a dominant personality to regard you as weak. Instead, act like the leader. Stand tall when you relate to your dog. Bend over him (not down to him) when you pet him. Always go first through doorways or up the stairs. Make him wait and then follow you. Always eat first before feeding your dog.

As the leader, you can give your dog permission to do things. For example, if he brings you a toy to throw for him, give him permission to do it, "Good boy to bring me your toy!" If he lies down at your feet by his own choice, tell him, "Good boy to lie down!" By giving him permission and praising him, you are putting yourself in control, even though he was already doing it of his own accord. Instead, it is a very

natural part of growing up. Keep in mind that this, too, shall pass. Your Dachshund will grow up someday. Adolescence typically lasts just a few months (in dogs, anyway).

GROWING UP

Dachshunds are not usually considered fully mature—mentally or physically—until they are two years old. And even then, some Dachshunds continue to behave like puppies for longer. Bitches (females) tend to act mature a little earlier than males.

After the teenage stage but before maturity, your Dachshund may go through another fear period. This hits at about 14 months of age, but may be later. Handle this one just like you did the others—don't reinforce your dog's fears. Happily, this is usually the last one he will have.

There may be another period of challenging—seeing if you really are the boss—at about two years of age. Treat this as you did the teenage stage; enforce the rules and praise what your dog does right.

When your Dachshund reaches his second birthday, throw a party! He is considered grown up now.

Early
PUPPY
Training

HOUSETRAINING

One of the most common methods of housetraining a puppy is paper training. The puppy is taught to relieve himself on newspapers and then, at some point, is retrained to go outside. Paper training teaches the puppy to relieve himself in the house. Is that really what you want your Dachshund to learn?

Teach your Dachshund what you want him to know now and later as an adult. Take him outside to the place where you want him to relieve himself and tell him, "Sweetie, go potty."

(Use any word you'll be comfortable saying.) When he has done what it is he needs to do, praise him.

Don't just open the door and send your puppy outside. How will you know that he has relieved himself? Go out with him so that you can teach him the command and can praise him when he does it. That way you'll know that he is done and that it's safe to let him back inside.

If he doesn't relieve himself when you take him outside, just put him back in his crate for a little while and take him back

Paper training is an effective method for housetraining your puppy, especially if you are not able to take him outside to relieve himself during the day.

Photo by Isabelle Francais

When it comes to correcting your Dachshund puppy, remember not to be too harsh. Behaviors that you might think are incorrect are perfectly natural to a dog.

BLANK SLATE

A young puppy's mind is like a blank slate or a newly formatted computer disk. What you teach your Dachshund puppy in his early months will have bearing on the puppy's behavior for the rest of his life. Therefore, it's important to keep in mind a vision of what your Dachshund will grow up to be.

outside later. Do *not* let him run around the house—even supervised—if he has not relieved himself outside.

Successful housetraining is based on setting your Dachshund puppy up for success rather than failure. Keep accidents to a minimum and praise him when he does relieve himself in the appropriate area.

CRATE TRAINING

By about five weeks of age, most puppies are starting to toddle away from their mother and littermates to relieve themselves. Using his instinct to keep his bed clean and with the help of a crate, you can housetrain your Dachshund puppy. A crate is a plastic or wire travel cage that can be used as your Dachshund's bed. Many new pet owners shudder at the thought of putting their puppy in a cage. "I could never do that!" they say. "It would be like putting my child in jail!" A puppy is not a child, however, and he has different needs and instincts. Puppies like to curl up in small dark places. That's why they like to sleep under the coffee table or under a chair.

dachshund

Because your Dachshund puppy has an instinct to keep his bed clean, being confined in the crate will help him to develop bowel and bladder control. When confined for gradually extended periods of time, he will hold his wastes to avoid soiling his bed. It is your responsibility to make sure he isn't left in his crate for too long.

The crate will also be your puppy's place of refuge. If he's tired, hurt, or sick, allow him to go back to his crate to sleep or hide. If he's overstimulated or excited, put him back in his crate to calm down.

Because the crate physically confines the puppy, it can also prevent some unwanted behaviors from occurring, such as destructive chewing or raiding the trash cans. When you cannot supervise the puppy or when you leave the house, putting him in his crate will prevent him from getting into trouble.

Introducing the Crate

Introduce your puppy to the crate by propping open the door and tossing a treat inside. As you do this, tell your puppy, "Go to bed!" When he goes inside to get the treat, let him investigate the crate and come

> ### PUNISHMENT
> Do not try to housetrain your puppy by punishing him for relieving himself in the house. If you scold him or rub his nose in his mess, you are not teaching him where he needs to relieve himself. You are, in effect, teaching him that you think going potty is wrong. Since he has to go, he will then become sneaky about it and you will find puddles and piles in strange places. Keep in mind that the act of relieving himself is very natural; he has to do this. Instead of concentrating on correction, emphasize praise for going in the right place.

and go as he wishes. Once he's comfortable with that, offer him his next meal in the crate and close the door behind him. Let him out when he's through eating. Offer several meals in the same fashion to show your puppy that the crate is a pretty neat place.

After your Dachshund puppy is used to going in and out for treats and meals, feed him back in his normal place again, but continue to offer a treat for going into the crate. Tell him, "Sweetie, go to bed," and then give him the treat.

Don't let your puppy out of the crate after a temper tantrum. If he starts crying, screaming, throwing himself at

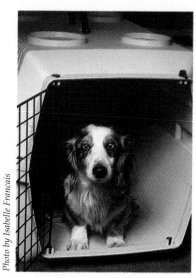

Photo by Isabelle Francais

A good way to introduce your puppy to the crate is by opening the door and putting a treat inside. Let him slowly get used to the crate until he is comfortable enough that you can close the door.

In these busy times, that is quality time.

Having you nearby will give your Dachshund puppy a feeling of security, whereas exiling him to the laundry room or backyard will isolate him. He will be more apt to cry, whine, chew destructively, or get into other trouble because of loneliness and fear.

Having the crate close by at night will save you some wear and tear, too. If he needs to go outside during the night (and he may need to for a few weeks), you will hear him whine and can let him out before he has an accident. If he's restless or bored, you can rap on the top of his crate and tell him to be quiet without getting out of bed.

Establish a Routine

Dachshunds, like many other dogs, are creatures of habit and thrive on a routine. Housetraining is much easier if there is a set routine for eating, eliminating, playing, walking, training, and sleeping. A workable schedule might look like this:

6:00 am—Dad wakes up and takes the puppy outside. After the puppy relieves himself, Dad praises him and brings him inside. He fixes the puppy's

the door, or scratching at the door, correct him verbally, "No, quiet!" or simply close the door to the room and walk away. If you let him out because of a tantrum, you will simply teach him that temper tantrums work. Instead, let him out when you are ready and when he is quiet.

Crate Location

The ideal place for the crate is in your bedroom, within arm's reach of the bed. This will give your Dachshund eight uninterrupted hours with you while you do nothing but sleep.

dachshund

breakfast, offers him water, and then sends him out into the backyard while he takes a shower.

7:00 am—Mom goes outside to play with the puppy for a few minutes before getting ready for work. Just before she leaves, she brings the puppy inside, puts him in his crate, and gives him a treat.

11:00 am—A dog-loving neighbor who is retired comes over, lets the puppy out of his crate, and takes him outside. The neighbor is familiar with the puppy's training, so he praises the puppy when he relieves himself. He throws the ball for the puppy, pets him, and cuddles him. When the puppy is worn out, he puts him back in his crate and gives him a treat.

3:00 pm—Daughter comes home from school and takes the puppy outside. She throws the ball for the puppy, picks up after him, and then takes him for a walk. When they get back, she brings the puppy inside to her bedroom while she does her homework.

6:00 pm—Mom takes the puppy outside to go potty, praises him, and then feeds him dinner.

8:00 pm—After Daughter plays with the puppy, she brushes him and takes him outside to go potty.

11:00 pm—Dad takes the puppy outside for one last trip before bedtime.

Any method of training will help your Dachshund's overall behavior. These two friends are a perfect example of good behavior.

dachshund

The schedule you set up will have to be compatible with your normal routine and lifestyle. Just keep in mind that your Dachshund puppy should not remain in the crate for longer than three to four hours at a time, except during the night. In addition, the puppy will need to relieve himself after waking up, eating, playtime, and every three to four hours in between.

Limit the Puppy's Freedom

Many puppies do not want to take the time to go outside to relieve themselves because everything exciting happens in the house. After all, that's

---

THERE ARE NO ACCIDENTS

If the puppy relieves himself in the house, it is not his fault. It's yours. That means the puppy was not well supervised or he wasn't taken outside in time. The act of relieving himself is very natural to the puppy, but the idea that there are certain areas where relieving himself is unacceptable is foreign to the puppy. His instincts tell him to keep his bed clean, but that's all. We need to teach him where we want him to go and prevent him from going in other places. That requires supervision on your part.

PATIENCE, PATIENCE, AND MORE PATIENCE

Dachshund puppies need time to develop bowel and bladder control. Establish a routine that seems to work well for you and for your puppy and then stick to it. Give your puppy time to learn and time to grow up. If you stick to the schedule, your puppy will progress. However, don't let success go to your head. A few weeks without a mistake doesn't mean your Dachshund puppy is housetrained; it means your routine is working. Too much freedom too soon will result in problems.

---

where all the family members are. If your Dachshund puppy is like this, you will find him sneaking off somewhere—behind the sofa or to another room—to relieve himself. By limiting the puppy's freedom, you can prevent some of these mishaps. Close bedroom doors and use baby gates across hallways to keep him close by. If you can't keep an eye on him, put him in his crate or take him outside.

HOUSEHOLD RULES

As mentioned, it's important to start teaching your Dachshund puppy the household rules that you wish him to follow as soon as

Photo by Isabelle Francais

A baby gate can prevent your Dachshund from getting into trouble. Also, remember to close bedroom doors when you can't supervise him.

dachshund

possible. Your eight- to ten-week-old puppy is not too young to learn. By starting early, you can prevent him from learning bad habits. When deciding which rules you want him to observe, look at your Dachshund puppy not as the baby he is now, but as the adult he will grow up to be. Do you want him to jump up on people? Do you want him to do that to the neighbor's children or to your grandmother?

Some of the rules you may want to institute could include teaching your Dachshund that jumping on people is not allowed, that he must behave when guests come to the house, that he should stay out of the kitchen, that he should leave the trash cans alone, and that he should chew only on his toys.

KEEP WALKING

Do you walk your dog when he has to go potty? Many dog owners live in condos and apartments and the dog must be taken for a walk in order to relieve himself. These dogs often learn that the walk is over once they go potty; therefore, they avoid going as long as possible so that the walk will continue. To avoid this trap, encourage your puppy to relieve himself right away, praise him, and then continue the walk or outing for a little while afterward.

Teaching your Dachshund puppy these rules is not difficult. Be very clear with your corrections. When he does something wrong, correct him in your deep, firm tone of voice, "No jump!" When he does something right, use a

Puppies depend on their owner for everything, including care and guidance. Patience and consistency are vital elements to successful housetraining.

Photo by Isabelle Francais

dachshund

Photo by Isabelle Francais

You want to teach your Dachshund puppy the household rules as soon as possible. By doing so, you can prevent him from learning poor habits. If your Doxie likes to jump, correct him in a deep, firm tone of voice, "No jump!"

puppy home, put a soft buckle collar on his neck. Make sure it's loose enough to come over his head in case he gets tangled up in something. Give him a day or two to get used to the collar. Then when you are going to be close by and can supervise him, snap the leash onto the collar and let him drag it behind him. As he walks around, he will step on the leash and feel it tug on his neck. In doing so, he will get used to the feel of it.

After two or three short sessions like this, you can teach

higher pitched tone of voice, "Good boy to chew on your toy!" You must be very clear—something is either right or it is wrong, there are no shades of gray.

ACCEPTING THE LEASH

Learning to accept the leash can be difficult for some puppies. If your Dachshund learns to dislike the leash as a young puppy, he may continue to resent it for many years. However, if he learns the leash is a key to more exciting things, he will welcome it.

Soon after you bring your

Guaranteed by the manufacturer to stop any dog of any size or weight from ever pulling again. It's like having power steering for your dog. Photo courtesy of Four Paws.

your puppy to follow you on the leash. Have a few pieces of a soft treat that your puppy enjoys (soft so that it can be easily chewed). Hold the leash in one hand and the treat in another. Show him the treat and back away a few steps as you tell your puppy, "Let's go! Good boy!" When he follows you a few steps, praise him and give him the treat. Dachshund puppies are usually very motivated by food, and when he learns a treat is being offered, he should follow you without a problem.

Repeat two or three times and then stop for this training session. Reward your puppy by giving him a tummy rub or by playing fetch.

After two or three training session like this, make it more challenging by backing up slowly or quickly or by making turns. If he gets confused or balks, make it simple until he's willingly following you again.

INTRODUCING THE CAR

Many puppies are afraid of the car because a ride in the car was the first strange thing to happen to them when they were taken from their mother and littermates. The car also takes them to the veterinarian's office, another strange place where someone in a white coat pokes them, prods them, and gives them vaccinations. You don't want this fear to grab hold, though; you want your puppy to understand that riding in the car is something fun to do.

To begin this exercise, start by lifting your puppy into the car and handing him a treat. As soon as he finishes the treat, lift him out of the car and walk away. Repeat this simple exercise several times a day for a few days. Next, lift him into the car, give him a treat, let him eat it, and then allow him to explore the car for a few minutes. After he has sniffed around, give him another treat, let him eat it, then lift him out and walk away. Continue this training for a week or two, depending on how nervous your puppy is in the car.

IF YOUR PUPPY BALKS

If your puppy balks, do not use the leash to drag him to you. This will cause him to dig his feet in and apply the brakes. Instead, kneel down, open your arms wide, and encourage him to come to you, "Hey, Sweetie, here! Good boy!" When he dashes into your lap, praise him and tell him what a wonderful puppy he is. Then try the exercise again.

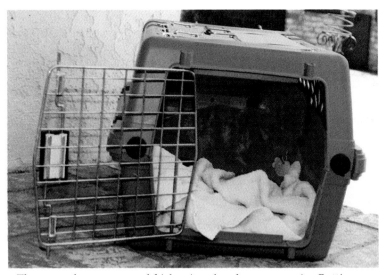

The car can be a strange and frightening place for some puppies. Putting your puppy in a travel crate will help him feel safe and secure while riding in the car.

Once your puppy is expecting a treat in the car, put his crate in the car and strap it down securely. Put your puppy in his crate, give him a treat, and then start the car's engine. Back down the driveway and then drive back up to the house. Stop the engine, give your puppy a treat, and then let him out of his crate and the car.

The next time drive down the street and back. Then go around the block. Increase the distances and times of the drives very gradually. Keep in mind that you want your puppy to expect good things in the car, not scary things. Your Dachshund puppy will have a lifetime of car rides ahead of

him, so life will be much nicer if he enjoys them.

SOCIAL HANDLING

Because your Dachshund puppy cannot care for himself, you must be able to brush and comb him, bathe him, check his feet for cuts and scrapes, and clean his ears. Your puppy doesn't understand why you need to do these annoying things to him and he may struggle when you try to care for him. This social handling exercise will help teach your puppy to accept your care.

Sit down on the floor with your puppy and have him lie down between your legs. He can lie on his back or on his

Photo by Isabelle Francais

Your Dachshund needs to be comfortable and relaxed while you groom him. Social handling exercises, such as giving him a slow tummy rub, will make him more cooperative.

dachshund

side; let him get comfortable. Start by giving him a slow, easy tummy rub. The idea here is to relax him. If your movements are fast and vigorous, you'll make him think that you want to play, so keep it slow and gentle. If he starts to struggle, tell him calmly, "Easy. Be still." Restrain him gently if you need to do so.

When your puppy is relaxed, start giving him a massage. Begin at his neck and ears, gently rubbing all around the base of each ear and working down the neck to the shoulders. Continue over his entire body, gently massaging it while at the same time checking his body for cuts, scratches,

END ON A HIGH NOTE
Always end these and all training sessions on a high note. If your Dachshund puppy is worried, scared, or confused, help him to do something right and then end the training session with praise. Never end a training session at a negative point in the training, or it will affect his outlook toward training later.

lumps, bumps, bruises, fleas, ticks, or any other problems that need to be attended to. Once your puppy has learned to enjoy this handling you can clean his ears, wash out his eyes, trim his toenails, or do anything else that needs doing during the massage.

If your Doxie puppy is full of energy, lie on the floor with him and give him a gentle massage. This will calm him down if he is overstimulated.

Photo by Isabelle Francais

dachshund

The Basic
OBEDIENCE
Commands

THE TEACHING PROCESS

Although Dachshunds are an intelligent breed, you cannot simply tell your Dachshund to do something and expect him to understand your words. Training is a process that begins with teaching your dog that certain words have meanings and that you would like him to follow your directions. Your Dachshund, however, won't understand why you want him to do these things; after all, why should he sit? He doesn't know why sitting is so important to you. Therefore, training is a process.

Show Your Dog

First, you need to show your dog what you want him to do and that there is a word—a human spoken sound—associated with that action or position. For example, when teaching him to sit, you can help him into position as you tell him, "Sweetie, sit." Follow that command with praise, "Good boy to sit!" even if you help him into position.

You will use a similar technique when teaching your dog most new things. If you want him to get off of the sofa, you can tell him, "Sweetie, off the furniture," as you take him by the collar and pull him off. When he's off of the furniture, tell him, "Good boy to get off of the furniture."

Praise

Praise him every time he does something right, even if you help him to do it. Your Dachshund will pay more attention and try harder if he is praised for his efforts. However, don't praise him when it's undeserved; Dachshunds are intelligent dogs and will quickly figure it out. Instead, give enthusiastic praise when he makes an effort and does something right for you.

Correct

Do not correct your dog until he understands what you want him to do. However, after he understands and is willing to obey the command and then chooses *not* to do it, correct him in a deep tone of voice, "Sweetie, no!" or a quick snap

Photo by Isabelle Francais

Showing your dog what you want him to do in addition to verbally telling him helps reinforce the command.

dachshund

Photo by Isabelle Francais

Remember to praise your Dachshund for correct behavior. He will try harder to please you if his efforts are rewarded.

USE INTERRUPTIONS

Interrupt incorrect behavior as you see it happen. If your dog is walking by the kitchen trash can and turns to sniff it, interrupt him, "Leave it alone!" If you tell him to sit and he does sit, but then starts to get up, interrupt him, "No! Sit." By interrupting him, you can stop incorrect behavior before or as it happens.

Interruptions and corrections alone will not train your Dachshund; they are used to stop—at that moment—undesirable behavior or actions. Your Dachshund learns much more when you reward his good behavior. Stop the behavior you don't want, but lavishly praise the actions you want to continue.

and release of the collar. Use *only* as much correction as is needed to get his attention and *no more*. With corrections, less is usually better as long as your dog is responding.

Your Timing

The timing of your praise, corrections, and interruptions is very important. Praise him *as* he is doing something right. Correct him *when* he makes the mistake. Interrupt him *as* he starts to stick his nose into the trash can. If your timing is slow, he may not understand what you are trying to teach him.

Be Fair

Dachshunds resent corrections that are too harsh

or unfair. They will show this resentment by refusing to work, by planting themselves and refusing to move, or by fighting back. An angry Dachshund has the potential to bite (even his owner) and that only compounds the problem. Make sure your training is fair.

SIT AND RELEASE

The sit command is the foundation for everything else your Dachshund will learn. When your dog learns to sit and sit still, he is learning to control himself. He is also learning that there are consequences to his actions. Learning to control himself and that he has control over the consequences to his actions is a very big lesson.

The sit command is also a good alternative action for problem behavior. Your Dachshund cannot sit still and jump on you at the same time. He can do one or the other; therefore, learning to sit still for praise can replace jumping up on people for attention. He can't be raking your leg with his nails or trying to knock his food bowl out of your hand if he's sitting still, waiting patiently for his dinner. You can fasten a leash to his collar more easily if he's sitting still. This is a practical, useful command.

As the foundation for most everything that your Doxie will learn, the sit command teaches him self-control. It's also a good alternative action for problem behavior.

There are two basic methods of teaching your Dachshund to sit. Some dogs do better with one technique than the other, so try both and see which works better for your Dachshund.

Hold your Dachshund's leash in your left hand and have some treats in your right hand. Tell him, "Sweetie, sit!" as you move your right hand (with the treats) from his nose, over his head, and toward his tail. He will lift his head to watch your hand. As his head goes up and back, his hips will go down. As he sits, praise him, "Good boy to sit!" and give him a treat. Pet him in the sitting position.

The release command lets your dog know when it is acceptable for him to get up from the sit position.

When you are ready for your dog to get up, tap him on the shoulder and tell him, "Release!" Each exercise needs a beginning and an end. The sit command is the beginning and the release command tells him that he is done and can now move. If he doesn't get up on his own, use his collar to walk him forward.

SIT, PLEASE!

Once your Dachshund understands the sit command and is responding well, have him sit for things that he wants. Have him sit when you hook his leash onto his collar before a walk. Have him sit before you give him a treat, give him his meals, or throw his ball.

ONE COMMAND

Don't keep repeating any command. For example, the command is not, "Sit! Sit, sit, *sit,* please sit. SIT!" If you give repeated commands for the sit, your Dachshund will assume that will apply to everything else. Tell him once to sit and then help him do it.

If your Dachshund is too excited by the treats to think (and some Dachshunds are like that), put the treats away. Tell your Dachshund to sit as you place one hand under his chin on the front of the neck and slide the other hand down his hips to tuck his back legs under him. Gently shape him into a sit as you give him the command, "Sweetie, sit." Praise him and release him.

If your dog is wiggly as you try to teach this exercise, keep your hands on him. If he pops up, interrupt that action with a deep, firm tone of voice, "Be still!" When he responds and stops wiggling, praise him quietly and gently.

DOWN

The down exercise continues one of the lessons the sit command started, self-control. Although it is hard for many energetic, bouncy young Dachshunds to control their

Although the stay command is somewhat difficult for an energetic Doxie to learn, it is a very important and useful lesson.

own actions, it is a lesson that all dogs must learn. Practicing the down exercise teaches your Dachshund to lie down and be still.

Start with your Dachshund in a sit. Rest one hand gently on his shoulder and hold a treat in the other hand. Let him smell the treat and then tell him, "Sweetie, down," as you take the treat straight down to the ground in front of his front paws. As he follows the treat down, use your hand on his shoulders to encourage him to lie down. Praise him, give him the treat, and then have him hold the position for a moment. Release him in the same way you did from the sit—pat him on the shoulder, tell him "Release!" and let him get up.

If your dog looks at the treat as you make the signal but doesn't follow the treat to the ground, simply scoop his front legs up and forward as you lay him down. The rest of the exercise is the same.

As your Dachshund learns what the down command means, you can have him hold it for a few minutes longer before releasing him—but do not step away from him yet. Stay next to him, and if he's wiggly, keep a hand on his shoulder to help him stay in position.

Once each day, have your Dachshund lie down and then

Before you release your Doxie from the down position, roll him over for a nice relaxing tummy rub. This will help him learn to enjoy the submissive position.

before releasing him, roll him over for a tummy rub. He will enjoy the tummy rub, relax a little, and learn to enjoy the down position. This is especially important for young Dachshunds that want to do anything *but* lie down and hold still.

Some Doxies with a more dominant personality— especially those that try to dominate their owner—will not want to lie down. The down is a more submissive position and these dogs will not want to willingly comply. For these dogs, try to turn the down into something fun—combine it with treats, meals, or tummy rubs instead of trying to force the

BE CLEAR

Make sure you are very clear in communicating to your dog what it is you want him to do. Remember that to your dog, something is either right or wrong—it's not partly right or partly wrong. Be fair with your commands, your praise, and your corrections.

dogs into complying. As mentioned, forceful training can turn into a fight and that's not the idea of training.

STAY

When your Dachshund understands both the sit and down commands, you can introduce him to the stay

Convey to your Dachshund that the word "stay" means "hold still." An open-hand gesture with the palm toward his face lets him know that you want him to remain in the stay position.

dachshund

exercise. You want to convey to your Dachshund that the word "stay" means "hold still." When your dog is sitting and you tell him to stay, you want him to remain in the sitting position until you go back to him and release him. When you tell him to stay while he's lying down, you want him to remain lying down until you go back to him to release him from that position. Eventually, he will be able to hold the sit position for several minutes and the down for even longer.

Begin the exercise by having your Dachshund sit. With the leash in your left hand, use it to exert a slight bit of pressure backward toward his tail as you tell him, "Stay." At the same time, use your right hand to give your dog a hand signal that will mean stay—an open-hand gesture with the palm toward your dog's face. Take one step away while releasing the pressure on the leash.

If your dog moves or gets up, tell him "No!" so that he knows he made a mistake and put him back into position. Repeat the exercise. After a few seconds, go back to him and praise him. Don't let him move from position until you release him.

Use the same process to teach the stay in the down

position. With the stay commands, you should always go back to your Dachshund to release him. Don't release him from a distance or call him to come to you from the stay position. If you do either of these, your dog will be much less reliable on the stay; he will continue to get up from the stay because you will have taught him to do exactly that. When teaching the stay, you want your Dachshund to learn that stay means "hold this position until I come back to you to release you."

As your Dachshund learns the stay command, you can *gradually* increase the time you ask him to hold the position. However, if your dog is making a lot of mistakes or moving often, you are either asking him to hold it for too long or he doesn't understand the command yet. In either case, go back and reteach the exercise from the beginning.

Increase the distance from your dog very gradually as well. Again, if your dog is making a lot of mistakes, you're moving away too quickly. Teach everything very gradually.

When your Dachshund understands the stay command but chooses not to do it, you

Remember to teach your dog the basic commands very gradually. If your Doxie is making mistakes or moving often, he may not completely understand the command. It's a good idea to go back and reteach the exercise.

dachshund

need to let him know the command is not optional. Many young, wiggly Dachshunds want to do anything but hold still; however, sitting still is very important to Dachshund owners. Correct excess movement first with your voice, "No! Be still! Stay!" and if that doesn't stop the excess movement, use a verbal correction and a snap and release of the leash. When he does control himself, praise him enthusiastically.

WATCH ME

The watch me exercise teaches your Dachshund to ignore distractions and pay attention to you. This is particularly useful when you're out in public and your dog is distracted by children playing or dogs barking behind a fence.

Start by having your Dachshund sit in front of you. Have a treat in your right hand. Let him sniff the treat and then tell him, "Sweetie, watch me!" as you take the treat from his nose up to your chin. When his eyes follow the treat in your hand and he looks at your face, praise him, "Good boy to watch me!" and give him the treat. Then release him from the sit. Repeat the exercise again exactly the same way two or

> ### USING THE STAY COMMAND
> You can use the stay command around the house. For example, in the evening while you're watching a favorite television show, have your Dachshund lie down at your feet while you sit on the sofa. Give him a toy to chew on and tell him, "Stay." Have him do a down/stay when your guests visit so that he isn't jumping all over them. Have him lie down and stay while the family is eating so that he isn't begging under the table. There are a lot of practical uses for the stay. Just look at your normal routine and see where this command can work for you.

three times and then quit for that training session.

Because this is hard for young, bouncing Dachshunds, practice it first at home where he can concentrate. Make sure your dog knows it well before you take him outside and try to practice it amid distractions. Take him out into the front yard (on leash, of course) and tell him to watch you. If he ignores you, take his chin in your left hand (treat is in the right) and hold it so that he looks at your face. Praise him even though you are helping him to do it.

When he will watch you outdoors with some

distractions, move on to the next step. Have him sit in front of you and tell him to watch you. As he watches you, take a few steps backward and ask him to watch you while walking. Praise him when he does. Try it again. When he can follow you six or seven steps and watch you at the same time, make it more challenging—back up and turn to the left or right, or back up faster. Praise him when he continues to watch you.

HEEL

You want your Dachshund to learn that heel means "walk by my left side, with your neck and shoulders by my left leg, and maintain that position." Ideally, your Dachshund should maintain that position as you walk slow, fast, turn corners, or weave in and out through a crowd.

To start, practice a "watch me" exercise to get your dog's attention on you. Back away from him and encourage him to watch you. When he does, simply turn your body as you are backing up so that your dog ends up on your left side and continue walking. If you have done it correctly, it is one smooth movement in which you and your dog end up walking forward together, with your dog on your left side.

The heel command teaches your dog to walk by your side and maintain that position whether you walk fast, slow, or turn corners.

Let's walk it through in slow motion. Sit your dog in front of you and do a "watch me." Back away from your dog and encourage him to follow you. When he's watching you, back up toward your left and as you are backing up, continue turning in that direction so you and your dog end up walking forward together. Your dog should end up on your left side (or you should end up on your dog's right side).

If your dog starts to pull forward, simply back away from him and encourage him to follow you. If you need to do so, use the leash with a snap and release motion to make the dog follow you. Praise him when he does.

Don't hesitate to go back and forth—walking forward and then backing away, walking forward and backing away—if you need to do so. In fact, sometimes this can be the best exercise you can do to get your dog's attention on you.

When your dog is walking nicely with you and paying attention to you, you can start to eliminate the backing away part of the exercise. Start the heel with your Dachshund sitting by your left side. Tell him, "Sweetie, watch me! Heel." Start walking. When he's walking nicely with you, praise him. However, if he gets distracted or starts to pull, simply back away from him again.

COME

The come command is one of the most important commands your Dachshund needs to learn. Not only is the come command important around the house in your daily routine, but it could also be a lifesaver someday, especially if your dog decides to dash toward the street when a car is coming. Because this command is so important, you will use

These eager Dachshunds demonstrate the come command, which is one of the most important commands that your dog needs to learn. You can teach the come command using treats or a sound stimulus.

two different techniques to teach your dog to come to you when you call him.

With a Treat

The first technique will use a sound stimulus and a treat to teach your Dachshund to come when you call him. Take a small plastic container (such as a margarine tub) and put a handful of dry dog food in it. Put the lid on and shake it. It should make a nice rattling sound.

Using treats is an effective way of teaching your Doxie to obey the come command, as demonstrated here.

Have the shaker in one hand and some good dog treats in the other. Shake the container, and as your Dachshund looks at it and you, ask him, "Sweetie, cookie?" Use whatever word he already knows for a treat. I use the word cookie, but you can use anything he already understands. When you say "Cookie," pop a treat in his mouth. Do it again. Shake, shake, "Sweetie, cookie?" and pop a treat in his mouth.

The sound of the container, your verbal question, and the treat are all becoming associated in his mind. He is learning that the sound of the container equals the treat—an important

lesson. Do this several times a day for several days.

Then, with your dog sitting in front of you, replace the word cookie with the word come. Shake the container, say "Sweetie, come!" and pop a treat in his mouth. You are rewarding him even though he didn't actually come to you—he was still sitting in front of you. However, you are teaching him that the sound of the shaker now equals the word come and he still gets the treat. Another

USING A SOUND STIMULUS

Do you remember those silent dog whistles that used to be advertised in comic books? There was nothing magical about those whistles, except that they were so high pitched that dogs could hear them but people couldn't. The container we are using to teach the come command works on the same principle that the silent dog whistle did—it's a sound stimulus that gets the dog's attention so that you can teach him. By getting him to pay attention to the sound of the shaker and by teaching him that the sound of the shaker means he's going to get a treat, you can make the come exercise that much more enticing. Your dog will be more likely to come to you (especially when there are distractions) if he's excited about it.

important lesson. Practice this several times a day for several days.

When your Dachshund is happy to hear the shaker and is drooling to get a treat, start calling him from across the room. Shake the container as you say, "Sweetie, come!" When he dashes to you, continue to give him a treat as you praise him, "Good boy to come!" Practice this up and down the hallway, inside and outside, and across the backyard. Make it fun, and keep up with the treats and the verbal praise.

With a Long Line

The second method to teach your dog to come uses a long leash or a length of clothesline rope. Because Dachshunds are athletic and fast (even with their short legs), you'll need a line at least 30 feet in length. Fasten the

DON'T USE THE COME COMMAND TO PUNISH

Never call your dog to come to you and then punish him for something he did earlier. Not only is the late punishment ineffective (it always is), but that unfair punishment will teach your dog to avoid you when you call him. Keep the come command positive all the time.

DON'T WORRY

Some people have reservations about this technique because they are worried that their dog will not come to them when they don't have a treat. First, you will use two different techniques to teach the come command and only one technique uses the treats. Second, even with this technique, you will eventually stop using treats. However, by using this technique when first introducing the come command, you can produce such a strong, reliable come response that it's worth all of your efforts.

line to your Dachshund's collar and then let him go play. When he is distracted by something, call him to come, "Sweetie, come!" If he responds right away, praise him.

If he doesn't respond right away, do *not* call him again. Pick up the line, back away from him, and by pulling the line, make him come to you. Do not give him a verbal correction at this time; he may associate the verbal correction with coming to you. Instead, simply make him come to you even if you have to drag him in with the line.

Let him go again and repeat the entire exercise. Make sure you always praise him when he

USE IT OR LOSE IT!

The best way to make this training work for you and your Dachshund is to use it. Training is not just for those training sessions; instead, training is for your everyday life. Incorporate it into your daily routine. Have your Dachshund sit before you feed him, or perform a down/stay while you eat, or a sit/stay at the gate while you take the trash cans out. Have him do a down/stay when guests come over. Use these commands as part of your life. They will work much better that way.

long line, especially in the early stages of training. You can always wean him from the treats later; right now, let's make the come command work.

Don't allow your Dachshund to have freedom off leash until he is grown up enough to handle the responsibility and is very well trained. Many dog owners let their dogs off leash much too soon and they learn bad habits that their owners wish they hadn't learned. Each time your dog learns that he can ignore you or run away from you, it reinforces the fact that he can. Instead, let him run around and play while dragging the long line. That way you can always regain control when you need to.

does decide to come to you. If he is very distracted, use the shaker and treats along with the

To avoid any accidents or mishaps, don't let your dog off leash before he is well trained enough to handle the responsibility.

Photo by Isabelle Francais

All About
FORMAL
Training

Many dog owners won't admit their dog needs training. "He does everything I ask," they say. Yet when asked specific questions about behavior, the answer changes. A trained Dachshund won't jump up on people, dash out the open door, or raid the trash can.

Dog owners benefit from training, too. During training, you learn how to teach your Dachshund and how to motivate him to be good so that you can encourage good behavior. You also learn how to

WHY IS TRAINING IMPORTANT?

When you decided to add a Dachshund to your family, you probably did so because you wanted a companion, a friend, and a confidant. You may have wanted a dog to go for walks with you, to run along the beach, to catch tennis balls, and to play with the kids. You may have wanted your children to have the same relationship with a dog that you remember from your childhood. To do any of these things, your Dachshund will need training.

Training your dog entails much more than the traditional sit, down, stay, and come commands. It's your responsibility to teach your Doxie that you set the rules and that he must follow them.

Photo by Isabelle Francais

prevent problem behavior from happening and how to correct mistakes when they do occur.

Dog training is much more than the traditional sit, down, stay, and come. It means teaching your Dachshund that he's living in your house and that you can set some rules he will be expected to follow. Training will not turn your Dachshund into a robot; instead, it will teach him to look at you in a new light and allow you to look at him differently, too. Training is not something you do *to* your Dachshund—it's something you do together.

TRAINING METHODS

Talk to 100 dog trainers (someone who trains dogs) or dog obedience instructors (someone who teaches the dog owner how to train his dog) about how they train and you will get 100 different responses. Any trainer or instructor who has been in the business for any period of time is going to work out a method or technique that works best for her. Each method will be based on the trainer's personality, teaching techniques, experience, and philosophy regarding dogs and dog training. Any given method may work wonderfully for one trainer, but

may fail terribly for another.

Because there are so many different techniques, styles, and methods, choosing a particular instructor may be difficult. It is important to understand some of the different methods so that you can make a reasonable decision.

Compulsive Training

Compulsive training is regarded as a method of instruction that forces the dog to behave. This is usually a correction-based training style, sometimes with forceful corrections. This type of training is generally used with law enforcement and military dogs and can be quite effective with hard-driving, strong-willed dogs. Many pet owners do not like this style of training and often feel it is too rough, especially for Dachshunds.

Inducive Training

This method of training is exactly the opposite of compulsive training. Instead of being forced to do something, the dog is induced or motivated toward proper behavior. Depending on the instructor, there are few or no corrections used. This kind of training works very well for most puppies, for softer dogs, and sometimes for owners who dislike corrections

Photo by Isabelle Francais

There are several different methods of dog training, including compulsive training and inducive training. It's your decision which method works best for you and your Dachshund.

dachshund

of any kind.

Unfortunately, this may not always be the right technique for all Dachshunds. Many Dachshunds will take advantage of the lack of corrections or discipline. Some very intelligent dogs with dominant personalities (including many Dachshunds) look upon the lack of discipline as weakness on your part and will set their own rules, which, unfortunately, may not be the rules you wish to enforce.

Somewhere in the Middle

A majority of trainers and instructors use a training method that is somewhere in between the inducive and compulsive techniques. An inducive method is used when possible, with corrections being used only as needed. Obviously, the range of techniques can be vast; some trainers will lean toward using more corrections, while others will use as few as possible.

FINDING AN INSTRUCTOR OR TRAINER

When trying to find an instructor or trainer, word-of-mouth referrals are probably the best place to start. Although anyone can place an

Finding a qualified instructor should be a priority when you decide to train your Doxie. Word-of-mouth referrals and your veterinarian are good sources of information.

dachshund

advertisement in the newspaper or yellow pages, the ad itself is no guarantee of quality or expertise. Happy customers are a good source of information and will demonstrate their experience with well-behaved dogs and will be glad to tell you where they received instruction.

Have you admired a neighbor's well-behaved dog? Ask where they went for training. Call your veterinarian, local pet store, or groomer for a recommendation. Make notes about each referral. What did people like about a particular trainer? What did they dislike?

Once you have a list of referrals, call each instructor and ask a few questions. How long has she been teaching classes? You will want someone with experience, of course, so that she can handle the various situations that may arise. However, experience alone is not the only qualification. Some trainers with years of experience are teaching exactly the same way as they did many years ago and have never learned anything new.

Ask the instructor about Dachshunds. What does she think of the breed? Ideally, she should be knowledgeable of the breed, what makes them tick,

and how to train them. If she doesn't like the breed—because Doxies can be so challenging, not all trainers like to train them—go elsewhere.

Ask the instructor to explain her training methods. Does this sound like something you would be comfortable with? If alternative methods are used, be aware that not every dog will respond the same way and that every instructor should have a backup plan.

Does the instructor belong to any professional organizations? The National Association of Dog Obedience Instructors (NADOI) and the Association of Pet Dog Trainers (APDT) are two of the more prominent groups. Both of these organizations publish regular newsletters to share information, techniques, new developments, and more. Instructors belonging to organizations such as these are more likely to be up-to-date on training techniques, styles, and so forth, as well as information about specific dog breeds.

Make sure, too, that the instructor will be able to help you achieve your goals. For example, if you want to compete in obedience trials, the instructor you choose should have experience in that

Training can help bring you and your dog closer together and build a stronger relationship.

specific field and knowledge of the rules and regulations concerning that competition.

After talking to several trainers or instructors, ask if you can watch their training classes. If a trainer says no, cross her off your list. There should be no reason why you cannot attend one class to see if you will be comfortable with this instructor and her style of teaching. As you watch the class, see how she handles the dogs. Would you let her handle your dog? How does she relate to the students? Are they relaxed? Do they look like they're having a good time? Are they paying attention to her?

After talking to the instructor or trainer, and after watching a class, you should be able to make a decision as to which class you want to attend. If you're still undecided, call the instructors back and ask a few more questions. After all, you are hiring someone to provide a service and you must be comfortable with your decision.

BUILDING A RELATIONSHIP

Training helps build a relationship between you and your dog. This relationship is built on mutual trust, affection, and respect. Training can also help your dog become your best friend and a well-behaved companion that is a joy to spend time with and one that won't send your blood pressure sky-high!

GROUP CLASSES OR PRIVATE LESSONS?

There are benefits and drawbacks to both group classes and private lessons. In group classes, the dog must learn to behave around other distractions, specifically the other dogs and people in class. Because the world is made up of lots of things capable of distracting your Dachshund, this can be beneficial. In addition, a group class can work like group therapy for dog owners. The owners can share triumphs and mishaps and can encourage and support one another. Many friendships have begun in group training classes.

The drawback to group classes is that the distractions of a large group are too much for some dogs. They simply cannot concentrate, especially in the beginning of training. For these dogs, a few private lessons may help to the extent that the dog can join a group class later. Dogs with severe behavior problems—especially aggression—should bypass group classes for obvious reasons.

Private lessons—one-on-one training with the owner, dog, and instructor—are also good for people with a very busy schedule who may otherwise not be able to do any training at all.

Puppy Class

Puppy or kindergarten classes are for puppies over 10 weeks of age but not over 16 weeks of age. These classes are usually half obedience training and half socialization, because to young pups, both of these subjects are very important. The owner also learns how to prevent problem behaviors

> ### GOALS FOR YOUR DACHSHUND
> What do you want training to accomplish? Do you want your Dachshund to be calm and well behaved around family members? Do you want him to behave himself in public places? Would you like to participate in dog activities and sports? There are an unlimited number of things you can do with your Dachshund—it's up to you to decide what you would like to pursue. Then you can find a training program to help you achieve those goals and have a trainer guide you in the right direction.

Whether you choose group training or private lessons for your Doxie, he will learn how to be a well-behaved and obedient companion.

ADVANCED TRAINING

Advanced training classes vary, depending on the instructor. Some offer classes to teach you to control your dog off leash, some emphasize dog sports, and others may simply continue basic training skills. Ask the instructor what kind of training classes she offers.

and his owner work on basic obedience commands, such as sit, down, stay, come, and heel. Most instructors will also spend time discussing problem prevention and problem solving, especially common problems like jumping on people, barking, digging, and chewing.

from occurring and how to establish household rules.

Basic Obedience Class

This class is for puppies that have graduated from a puppy class, for puppies over four months of age that haven't attended a puppy class, or for adult dogs. In this class, the dog

Dog Sports Training

Some instructors offer training for one or more dog activities or sports. There are classes to prepare you for competition in obedience trials, conformation dog shows, flyball, agility, or hunting field trials. Other trainers may offer training for noncompetitive activities, such as therapy dog work.

You can determine what type of training class your puppy should be in by his age. Puppies between 10 and 16 weeks of age should be in a puppy class; basic obedience class is for puppies that are ready for more advanced training.

Photo by Isabelle Francais

dachshund

Problem
PREVENTION
and Solving

Dachshunds, unfortunately, can be unusually destructive puppies. Their high activity level, tremendous energy, playfulness, and intelligence just seem to combine long enough to get them into trouble. But just because this *can* happen doesn't mean you have to allow it to happen—you can prevent problems from occurring.

Many of the behaviors that dog owners consider problems—including destructiveness, barking, digging, chewing, jumping up on people, and so on—aren't problems to your Dachshund. In fact, they are very natural behaviors to your dog. Dogs dig because the dirt smells good or because there's a gopher in the yard. They bark

You might consider certain behaviors, such as barking, digging, or jumping up on people to be problems. Although most of these behaviors are natural to your dog, training can help prevent or keep these actions under control.

Photo by Isabelle Francais

to verbalize something, just as people talk. All of the things you consider problem behaviors are very natural behaviors to your dog. However, most problem behavior can be worked with and either prevented, controlled, or in some cases, stopped entirely.

WHAT YOU CAN DO

Prevent Problems From Happening

Because so many of the things we consider problems are natural behaviors to your Dachshund, you need to prevent as many of them from happening as you reasonably can. Put the trash cans away so that he never discovers that the kitchen trash is full of good tasting surprises. Make sure the kids put their toys away so that your Dachshund can't chew them to pieces. It's much easier to prevent a problem from happening than it is to break a bad habit later.

Preventing a problem from happening might require that you fence off the garden, build higher shelves in the garage, or perhaps build a dog run for your Dachshund.

Preventing problems from occurring also requires that you

> ### TRAINING
> Training can play a big part in controlling problem behavior. A fair, upbeat, yet firm training program teaches your dog that you are in charge—that he is below you in the family pack. The training should also reinforce his concept of you as a kind, calm, caring leader. In addition, training skills give you the ability to teach your dog what is acceptable and what is not.

You can prevent problems from occurring by simply limiting your dog's freedom. Large crates or baby gates are effective tools for preventing unnecessary accidents.

Photo by Isabelle Francais

dachshund

A DOG RUN

A dog run is not a dog prison; instead, it is a safe place for him to stay while he's unsupervised. In his dog run, he should have protection from the sun and weather, unspillable water, and a few toys. Don't put him in his run as punishment and never scold him while he is in it. Whenever you put him in his run, give him a treat or a toy and leave a radio on in a nearby window playing quiet, elevator-type music.

limit your dog's freedom. A young puppy or untrained dog should never have unsupervised free run of the house; there is simply too much he can get into. Instead, keep him close to you and close off rooms. If you can't watch him, put him into his run or out in the backyard.

Health Problems

Some experts feel that 20 percent of all commonly seen behavior problems are caused by health-related problems. A bladder infection or a gastrointestinal upset often causes housetraining accidents. Medications can cause behavior changes. Thyroid problems can cause a behavior change, as can hyperactivity, hormone imbalances, and a variety of other health problems.

If your dog's behavior changes, make an appointment with your veterinarian. Tell him

Despite what some people believe, a dog run is not a prison. It's a safe place for your dog to stay when you can't supervise him that allows him to play and exercise.

Photo by Isabelle Francais

dachshund

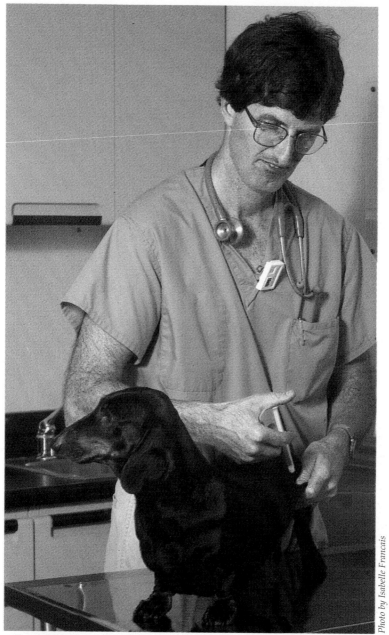

Photo by Isabelle Francais

If your Doxie's behavior suddenly changes, it could be the result of a health problem. If this is the case, make an appointment with your veterinarian immediately before starting corrections.

dachshund

why you are bringing the dog in, don't just ask for an exam. Explain that your Dachshund has changed his behavior, tell your vet what the behavior is, and ask if he could do an exam of any physical problems that could lead to that type of behavior.

Don't automatically assume your dog is healthy. If a health problem is causing the behavior change, training or behavior modification won't make it better. So before beginning any training, talk to your veterinarian. Once health problems are ruled out, you can start working on the problem.

Nutrition

Nutrition can play a part in causing or solving behavior problems. If your dog is eating poor-quality food or if he cannot digest the food he is being fed, his body may be missing some vital nutrients. If your Dachshund is chewing on rocks or wood, chewing the stucco off the side of your house, or grazing on the plants in your garden, he may have a nutritional deficiency of some kind.

Some dogs develop a type of hyperactivity when fed a high-calorie, high-fat dog food. Other dogs have food allergies that may show up as behavior problems.

If you have any questions about the food your dog is eating, talk to your veterinarian.

Play

Play is different from exercise, although exercise can

The use of better ingredients in your dog's food leads to better nutrition and therefore to better health. Make sure the dog food you choose contains only the highest quality ingredients. Photo courtesy of Nutro Products, Inc.

be play. The key to play is laughter. Researchers know that laughter is wonderful medicine; it makes you feel better. When you laugh, you feel differently about the world around you.

Laughter and play have a special place in your relationship with your Dachshund. Doxies can be very silly and you should take advantage of that—laugh at him and with him. Play games that will make both of you laugh.

Play is also a great stress reliever. Make time for play when you are having a hard time at work. Play with your Dachshund after training sessions.

Sometimes dogs get into trouble intentionally because they feel ignored. To these dogs, any attention—even corrections or yelling—is better than no attention at all. If you

Proper nutrition is imperative to your dog's health. Veterinarians recommend elevated feeders to help reduce stress on your dog's neck and back muscles. The raised platform also provides better digestion while reducing bloating and gas. Photo courtesy of Pet Zone Products, Ltd.

take time regularly to play with your dog you can avoid some of these situations.

DEALING WITH SPECIFIC PROBLEMS

Jumping on People

Just about every Dachshund owner, at one time or another, has to deal with their dog jumping up on people. Perhaps it is because the Doxie has short legs that he feels he must jump high. Whatever the reason, you can control the jumping by emphasizing the sit. If your Dachshund is sitting, he can't be jumping up. By teaching him to sit for petting, praise, treats, and meals, you can teach him that the sit is important and that everything he wants will

happen only when he sits.

Use the leash as much as you can to teach your Dachshund to sit. Small but solid, muscular dogs, Dachshunds can be tough to hold onto unless you have something to grab a hold of, and the leash is your best training tool. When you come home from work, don't greet your dog until you have a leash and collar in hand. As your dog greets you, slip the leash over his head. Then you can help him sit. If he tries to jump, use a snap and release of the leash and a verbal correction, "No jump! Sit!" Of course, as with all of your training, praise him when he sits.

When you are out in public, make sure your Dachshund sits before any of your neighbors or

Dachshunds are natural hunters, so it's not unusual for them to dig in your backyard. You can prevent this behavior by building your pet a dog run where he can have the freedom to do as he pleases.

Photo by Isabelle Francais

friends pet him. Again, use your leash. If he won't sit still, don't let anyone pet him, even if you have to explain your actions. "I'm sorry, but I'm trying to teach him manners and he must sit before he gets any petting," should be enough explanation.

The key to correcting a dog when he jumps up is to make sure the bad behavior is not rewarded. If someone pets your Dachshund when he jumps up, that action has been rewarded. However, receiving all of the attention when he's sitting will make sitting that much more attractive to him.

Digging

It's amazing how much earth one short-legged, little dog can move! Dachshunds were bred to hunt for their prey in burrows and tunnels, so being

All dogs need exercise, training, and playtime on a daily basis to use up their excess energy and stimulate their mind.

Photo by Isabelle Francais

underground is perfectly natural to them. This makes correcting his digging a difficult project. If your backyard looks like a military artillery range, you need to concentrate first on preventing this problem from occurring. If you come home from work to find new holes in the lawn or garden, don't correct him then. He probably dug the holes when you left in the morning and a correction ten hours later won't work.

Instead, build a dog run for him and leave him there during the day. If you fence off one section of your yard alongside your house, you might be able to give him a run that is 6 feet wide by 20 feet long. That's a great run. Let him trash this area to his heart's content; that's his yard. Just make sure he can't dig under the fence.

Then, when you are home and can supervise him, you can let him have free run of the rest of your yard. When he starts to get into trouble, you can use your voice to interrupt him, "Hey! What are you doing? Get out of the garden!"

The destructive dog also needs exercise, training, and playtime every day to use up his energy, stimulate his mind, and spend time with you. Most importantly, don't let this dog watch you garden. If you do, he may come to you later with all of those bulbs you planted earlier.

The Barker

Dachshunds are not normally problem barkers, although they can bark quite a bit (and loudly) when defending their home and yard from real or imagined trespassers. A Dachshund left alone for many hours each day may find that barking and howling gets him attention, especially if your neighbors yell at him. To your Dachshund,

negative attention is better than no attention at all.

Start teaching your dog to be quiet when you're at home with him. When your Dachshund starts barking, tell him, "Quiet!" When he stops, praise him. When he understands what you want, go for a short walk outside, leaving him home. Listen, and when you hear him start to bark, come back and correct him. After a few corrections, when he seems to understand, ask your neighbor to help you. Go outside and ask your neighbor to join you for a

Giving your dog a treat or toy when you leave the house can distract him, thus reducing barking or whining.

conversation. Have the kids outside playing. When your dog barks because he's feeling left out, go back and correct him. Repeat as often as you need to until he understands.

You can reduce your dog's emotional need to bark if you make coming home and leaving home quiet and low keyed. When you leave the house, don't give him hugs or tell him repeatedly to be a good dog. That simply makes your leaving more emotional. Instead, give him attention an hour or two prior to your leaving, and when it's time for you to go, just go. When you come home, ignore your dog for a few minutes. Then whisper hello to him. Your Dachshund's hearing is

very good, but to hear your whispers he is going to have to be quiet and still.

You can also distract your dog when you leave. Take a brown paper lunch bag and put a couple of treats in it, maybe a dog biscuit, a piece of carrot, and a slice of apple. Roll the top over to close it and rip a very tiny hole in the side of the bag to give your dog encouragement to get the treats. As you walk out the door or gate, hand this to your dog. He will be so busy figuring out where the treats are and how to get them, he'll forget you are leaving.

Dashing Through Doors and Gates

This is actually one of the easier behavior problems to solve. Train your Dachshund to sit at all doors and gates, then to hold that sit position until you give him permission to go

ONE DACHSHUND OR TWO?

If you are gone for many hours each day, you may want to get a second Dachshund to keep your first dog company. Granted, two dogs *are* twice as much work as one, but Dachshunds are pack dogs and a dog left alone for most of the day is going to be unhappy. Two dogs can keep each other occupied and reduce your feelings of guilt.

Photo by Isabelle Francais

Because Dachshunds are pack dogs, they prefer to be in the company of one another. These two Doxies spell "double trouble."

dachshund

through or to get up after you have gone through. By teaching him to sit and to wait for permission, you will eliminate the problem.

Start with your dog on leash. Walk him up to a door. Have him sit, tell him to stay, and then open the door in front of him. If he dashes through, use the leash to correct him (snap and release) as you give him a verbal correction, "No! Stay!" Take him back to his original position and do it again. When he will hold his position at the door, go to another door or gate and repeat the training procedure.

When he will wait while on leash at all doors and gates, take the leash off and hook up his long line. Fasten one end of the long line to a piece of heavy furniture. Walk him up to a door and tell him to sit and stay. Drop the long line to the ground. With your hands empty, open the door and stand aside. Because your hands are empty (meaning you aren't holding the leash), your Dachshund may decide to dash. If he does, the long line will stop him or you can step on the line. Give him a verbal correction, too, "No! I said stay!" and bring him back to where he started. Repeat the training session here and at all other doors and gates.

RUNNING FREE

If your Dachshund does make it out through a door or gate, don't chase him. The more you chase him, the better the game is, as far as he's concerned. Instead, use your shaker for training the come command. Shake it, "Sweetie, do you want a cookie? Come!" When he comes back to you, you must praise him for coming even though you may want to wring his neck for dashing through the door. Don't correct him, a correction will make him avoid you even more the next time it happens.

Other Problems

Many behavior problems can be solved or at least controlled by using similar techniques. Try to figure out why your Dachshund is doing what he's doing from his point of view, not yours. What can you do to prevent the problem from happening? What can you do to teach your dog not to do it? Remember, as with all of your training, a correction alone will not change the behavior; you must also teach your dog what he can and can't do.

If you still have some problems or if your dog is showing aggressive tendencies, contact your local dog trainer or behaviorist for some help.

Advanced
TRAINING
and Dog Sports

If you and your Dachshund enjoyed the time you spent together while training, it doesn't have to be over just because you have completed the basic obedience course. There is always more to learn. You can teach your dog to listen to you off leash, teach him hand signals, or perhaps teach him some tricks. There is a lot you can do together, including a number of different dog activities and sports. However, before you begin any of these exercises or activities, make sure your Dachshund is proficient in all of the basic commands. If he's having trouble with some of the commands, go back, review them, and practice them.

HAND SIGNALS

When you start teaching hand signals, have a treat in your hand to get your Dachshund's attention. Use the verbal command he already knows to help him understand what you are trying to tell him. As he responds, decrease the verbal command to a whisper and emphasize the hand signal.

USING HAND SIGNALS

Dog owners often think that hand signals are something that only really advanced dogs can respond to and that is partly right. It does take some training. However, hand signals can be useful for all dog owners. For example, if your dog learns to respond to hand signals, you can give him the signal to go lie down while you're talking on the telephone without having to interrupt your conversation.

Using hand signals in conjunction with verbal commands helps your Doxie to better understand what you want him to do.

The difficult part of teaching hand signals is that, at first, your dog may not understand that these movements of your hand and arm have any significance. After all, people "talk" with their hands all the time; they are always moving and waving. Dogs learn early to ignore hand and arm movements. Therefore, to make hand signals work, your Dachshund needs to watch you. A good treat in the hand making the movement can help.

Down

When you taught your Dachshund to lie down by taking a treat from his nose to the ground in front of his front paws, you were teaching him a hand signal. Granted, he was watching the treat in your hand, but he was also getting used to seeing your hand move. Therefore, switching him from a verbal command to a hand-signal-only command should be easy.

Have your dog sit in front of you. Verbally, tell him "Down" as you give him the hand signal for down with a treat in your hand, just as you did when you were originally teaching it. When he's down, praise him and then release him. Practice it a few times.

Now, give him the signal to go down (with a treat in your hand), but do not give a verbal command. If he lies down,

Once your dog can reliably follow your signal for down without a verbal command, you can make it more challenging. For example, signal him to lie down when you are across the yard from him.

dachshund

praise him, give him the treat, and release him. If he does not go down, give the leash a slight snap and release down toward the ground—not hard—but just enough to let him know, "Hey! Pay attention!" When he goes down, praise him and release him.

When he can reliably follow the signal without a verbal command, make it more challenging. Signal him to lie down when you are across the room from him. Signal him to lie down while you're talking to someone. Signal him to lie down when there are some distractions around him. Remember to praise him enthusiastically when he goes down on the signal.

Sit

If you were able to teach your Dachshund to sit using the treat above his nose, you were teaching him to sit using a hand signal. If you had to teach him by shaping him into a sit, don't worry, we can still teach him a signal.

With your Dachshund on leash, hold the leash in your left hand and have a treat in your right hand. Stand in front of your Dachshund and take the treat from his nose upward and over his head. At the same time,

This Doxie obediently sits on command.

whisper "Sit." When he sits, praise him and release him. Try it again. When he is reliably watching your hand and sitting, stop whispering the command and let him follow the signal. If he doesn't sit, jiggle the leash and collar to remind him that something is expected. Again, when he sits, praise him.

Stay

When you taught the stay command you used a hand signal, the open-palm gesture toward your Dachshund's face. This signal is so obvious your dog will probably do it without any additional training. Have your dog sit or lie down and tell him "Stay" using only the hand signal. Did he hold it? If he did, go back to him and praise him.

If he didn't, use the leash to correct him (snap and release) and try it again.

Come

You want the signal for the come to be a very broad, easily seen signal, one that your dog can recognize even if he's distracted by something. Therefore, this signal will be a wide swing of the right arm, starting with your arm held straight out from your side at shoulder height and horizontal to the ground. The motion will be to bring the hand to your chest following a wide wave—as if you were reaching out to get your dog and bring him to you.

Start the signal by having the come shaker in your right hand. Shake it slightly to get your dog's attention and then complete the signal. Praise your dog when he responds and comes to you.

If he doesn't respond right away, start the signal again and this time verbally tell him to come as you are making the signal and shaking the shaker. Again, praise him when he comes. Gradually eliminate the verbal command, and when your Dachshund is responding well, gradually stop using the shaker as well.

OFF-LEASH CONTROL

One of the biggest mistakes many dog owners make is to take their dog off the leash too soon. When you take your dog off his leash you have very little control; only your previous training can control him. If you take your dog off leash before you have established enough control or before your dog is mentally mature enough to accept that control, you are setting yourself up for disaster.

Dachshunds are smart, curious dogs, and they love to check out new things, especially new smells. A rabbit, butterfly, or bird was made to chase as far as Doxies are concerned. More than one Dachshund has been so involved in his exploring that he's forgotten to pay attention to his owner's commands.

Before your Dachshund is allowed off leash outside of a fenced yard or your backyard, you need to make sure his training is sound—which means he should be responding reliably and well to all of the basic commands.

Your dog must also be mentally mature, and in some Dachshunds that might be at two or even two and a half years of age. He should be past the challenging teenage stage of development. Never take a young adolescent off leash outside of a fenced-in area; that would be setting a young dog up for problems.

Come on a Long Line

The long line (or leash) was introduced earlier in the section on teaching the come command. It is also a good training technique for preparing your dog for off-leash control. Review that section and practice it until you are comfortable that your dog understands the come command from 20 to 30 feet away (the length of the long line) and will do it reliably.

Now take your dog out to play in a different place that is safe and free from danger—a schoolyard is good. Let your Dachshund drag his long line behind him as he sniffs and explores. When he's distracted and not paying attention to you, call him to come. If he responds right away, praise him enthusiastically. Tell him what a smart, wonderful dog he is.

If he doesn't respond right away, step on the end of the long line, pick it up, and back away from your dog, calling him again as you use the long line to make him come to you. Don't beg him to come to you or repeat the come command over and over again. Simply use

Retractable leashes provide dogs freedom while allowing the owner complete control. Leashes are available in a wide variety of lengths for all breeds of dogs. Photo courtesy of Flexi-USA, Inc.

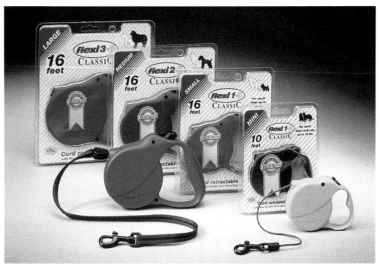

the line to make him do it. The come is not an optional command.

Heel

Most places require that dogs be leashed in public. However, teaching your Dachshund to heel without a leash is a good exercise. Not only is it a part of obedience competition (for people interested in that sport), but it's a good practical command, too. What would happen if your dog's leash or collar broke when you were out for a walk? Accidents do happen, and if your dog has already been trained to heel off leash, disaster can be averted!

Eventually, you want your dog to be able to walk nicely by your side without a leash. This Doxie is still in training.

To train for this, hook two leashes up to your dog's collar. Use your regular leash and a lightweight leash. Do a watch me exercise with treats and then tell your dog to heel. Practice a variety of things— walk slowly, quickly, turn corners and perform figure eights. When your dog is paying attention well, reach down and unhook his regular leash, tossing it to the ground in front of him. If he bounces up assuming he's free, correct him with the second leash, "Hey! I didn't release you!" and make him sit in the heel position. Hook his regular leash back up and repeat the exercise.

When he doesn't take advantage of the regular leash being taken off, tell him to heel and start practicing the heel exercise. Do not use the second leash for minor corrections, save it for control. If he tries to dash away, pull from you, or otherwise break the heel exercise, use that second leash and hook his regular leash back on again.

Repeat this exercise, going back and forth between one leash and two, until he's not even thinking about whether or not his regular leash is on. You want him to work reliably without questioning the leash's control. For some Dachshunds, this may take several weeks worth of work.

When your Dachshund is working reliably, put the second leash away. Take his regular leash, hook it up to his collar, and fold it up. Tuck it under his collar between his shoulder blades so that it is lying on his back. Practice his heel work. If he makes a mistake, grab the leash and collar as a handle and correct him. When the correction is over, remove your hand from the collar.

Expect and demand the same level of obedience off leash that you do on leash. Don't make excuses for off-leash work.

DOG SPORTS

Do you like training your Dachshund? If you and your Dachshund are having a good time, you may want to try one or more dog activities or sports. There are a lot of different things you can do with your dog—some are competitive, some are fun, some do good works. What you decide to do depends on you and your dog.

Conformation Competition

The American Kennel Club (AKC) and the United Kennel Club (UKC) both award conformation championships to purebred dogs. The

Participating in various sports can be a lot of fun for both you and your Dachshund. It's up to you to decide if you want to be competitive or just have fun.

Photo by Isabelle Francais

dachshund

requirements vary between the registries, but basically a championship is awarded when a purebred dog competes against other dogs of his breed and wins. When competing, the judge compares each dog against a written standard for his breed and chooses the dog that most closely represents that standard of excellence.

This is a very simplistic explanation. However, if you feel that your Dachshund is very handsome and that you might want to compete, go watch a few local dog shows. Observe the Dachshunds competing and talk to some of their owners and handlers. Does your Dachshund still look like a good candidate? You will also want to do some reading about your breed and about conformation competition, and perhaps attend a conformation class.

Obedience Competition

Obedience competition is a team sport involving you and your Dachshund. There are set exercises that must be performed in a certain way, and both you and your dog are judged as to your abilities to perform these exercises.

Both the AKC and the UKC sponsor obedience competitions

FIELD TRIALS

Dachshunds are hunting dogs, and to a Dachshund, there is nothing better than chasing a rabbit! If you would like to work with your Dachshund in his instinctive occupation, write to the American Kennel Club or the Dachshund Club of America and ask for information about Dachshund field trials. You can also contact a dog trainer in your area and ask if someone is training field hounds locally. Dachshund breeders may also be able to refer you to a field trainer.

---

for all breeds of dog, as do some other organizations, including the Dachshund Club of America. Independent obedience competitions or tournaments are also held all over the country.

Before you begin training to compete, write to the sponsoring organization and get a copy of the rules and regulations pertaining to competition. Go to a few local dog shows and watch the obedience competitions to see which dogs win and which don't. What did they each do differently? There are also a number of books on the market specifically addressing obedience competition. You may want to find a trainer in your area who specializes in competition training.

dachshund

Canine Good Citizen

The Canine Good Citizen (CGC) program was instituted by the AKC in an effort to promote and reward responsible dog ownership. During a CGC test, the dog and owner must complete a series of ten exercises, including sitting for petting and grooming, walking nicely on the leash, sit, down, stay, and come. Upon the successful completion of all ten exercises, the dog is awarded the title "CGC."

For more information about CGC tests, contact a dog trainer or dog training club in your area.

AGILITY

Agility is a fast-paced sport in which the dog must complete a series of obstacles correctly in a certain period of time, with the fastest time winning. Obstacles might include tunnels, hurdles, an elevated dog walk, and more. The AKC, the UKC, and the United States Dog Agility Association all sponsor agility competitions. Dachshunds do participate in agility for fun and training, although having short legs makes it hard for them to be competitive against faster breeds like Border Collies and Shetland Sheepdogs.

One of the main qualifications for winning the Canine Good Citizen (CGC) title is the ability to get along with other dogs. This trio of Doxies looks like they're the best of friends.

Photo by Isabelle Francais

dachshund

Photo by Isabelle Francais

If you are going to own more than one dog, it's important that they all get along peacefully.

Temperament Test

The American Temperament Test Society was founded to provide breeders and trainers with a means of uniformly evaluating a dog's temperament. By using standardized tests, each dog would be tested in the same manner. The tests can be used to evaluate potential or future breeding stock, future working dogs, or can simply

Because of their excellent scenting abilities, Dachshunds make exceptional tracking dogs.

Photo by Isabelle Francais

dachshund

be a way for dog owners to see how their dog might react in any given situation.

For information about temperament tests in your area, contact a local trainer or dog training club.

Tracking

Dachshunds have exceptional scenting abilities and make excellent tracking dogs. The American Kennel Club sponsors tracking competitions. For more information, write to the AKC and ask for their rules

Most researchers agree that dogs are great therapy for people who need extra love and affection. If you feel that your Doxie has a special gift, contact your local dog trainer for information about a therapy group in your area.

> ### FLYBALL
> Flyball is a great sport for dogs that are crazy about tennis balls. This team sport involves two teams of four dogs and their owners competing against one another. The dogs—one on each team at a time—run down the course, jump four hurdles, and then trigger a mechanism that spits out a tennis ball. The dogs then turn, jump the four hurdles again, and return to their owner. The team to complete the relay first, wins. Dachshunds can participate in flyball and have a great time, but again, short legs make it hard for a Doxie to compete against some of the more athletic breeds. However, flyball is a fun sport and great exercise for any dog.

and regulations concerning tracking trials.

Therapy Dogs

Dog owners have known for years that our pets are good for us, but now researchers are agreeing—dogs are good medicine. Therapy dogs go to nursing homes, hospitals, and children's centers to provide warmth, affection, and love to the people who need it most. Dachshunds are sometimes a little standoffish with strangers, but the ones that like people make great therapy dogs. Contact your local dog trainer for information about a group in your area.

Photo by Isabelle Francais

Have Some
FUN
With Your Training

Obedience training has a tendency to be serious; after all, much of this training is teaching your Dachshund what his place is in the family and how to control himself. However, training can also be fun, especially from a Dachshund's viewpoint. Games and trick training can challenge your training skills and your Dachshund's ability to learn. Once you have taught your dog, you can have a great time showing off his tricks, amusing your friends, and just plain having fun with your pet.

TRACKING FOR FUN

Most dog owners assume that tracking is something that search and rescue dogs or law enforcement dogs do to find or save people. And it's true; these dogs need tracking skills. But tracking can also be fun for you and your Dachshund and can be something you practice as a game.

Go out to your yard or to an empty schoolyard or vacant lot first thing in the morning. Put a chest harness (not a neck collar that could hamper his movements) on your Dachshund

and fasten a leash to it. Rub a piece of hot dog on the sole of one shoe and then rub that shoe in the grass, imparting the smell to the grass. Walk forward 20 or 30 feet, scuffing that foot a little, and then place a bit of hot dog on the ground. Jump off your track (a big jump to the side if you're able) and walk back to your dog.

THE COME GAME

The come game is a great way to show your Dachshund puppy how much fun it is to come when called. The game begins with two family members seated on the ground or floor across the yard or down the hallway from each other. Each should have some treats for the puppy. One family member can call the puppy from across the yard (or down the hall), and when the puppy reaches her, she should praise the puppy and give him a treat. She can then turn the puppy around so that he's facing the other family member, who can then call the puppy. This very simple game can make teaching the come command exciting for the puppy. In addition, kids can play this game with the puppy, giving them a chance to participate in the puppy's training.

Photo by Isabelle Francais

Teaching your Dachshund different tricks can be fun. It also challenges your training skills and your dog's ability to learn.

Point to the ground where you started as you tell your dog, "Find it!" When he starts sniffing, let him work it out. As he starts following the track, hold the leash but let him move ahead of you—don't interfere. When he finds the treat, praise him.

As he gets better, you can make the track more difficult by adding turns or zigzags. Use the hot dogs for quite a while, though, to make the tracking more fun for him.

RETRIEVING

Most Dachshunds like to retrieve; they just don't always understand the need to bring back what they go out after! However, once you teach your Dachshund to bring back their toy, retrieving games can be great fun, as well as good exercise.

If your Dachshund likes to retrieve, then all you need to do is get him to bring the toy back to you. When you throw the toy and he goes after it, wait until he picks it up. Once he has it in his mouth, call him back to you in a happy tone of voice. If he drops the toy, send him back to it. If he brings the toy all the way back to you, praise him enthusiastically.

Don't let him play tug-of-war with the toy. If he grabs it and doesn't want to let go, reach over the top of his muzzle and tell him "Give," as you press his top lips against his teeth. You don't have to use much pressure, just enough so that he opens his mouth to relieve the pressure and release the toy. When he gives you the toy, praise him.

If your Dachshund likes to take the toy and run with it, let him drag his long line behind him while he plays. Then, when he dashes off, you can step on the line and stop him. Once you've stopped him, call him back to you.

THE NAME GAME

The name game is a great way to make your dog think. And don't doubt him for a minute; your Dachshund can think! When you teach your Dachshund the names of a variety of things around the house, you can put him to work, too. Tell him to pick up your keys or your purse or send him after the remote control to the television. The possibilities are unlimited.

Begin with two items that are very different, perhaps a tennis ball and a magazine. Sit on the floor with your Dachshund and place the two items in front of you. Ask him, "Where's the ball?" and bounce the ball so that he tries to grab it or at least pays attention to it. When he touches it, praise him and give him a treat.

When he is responding to the ball, roll it on the floor and send him after it. Praise and reward him. Now set several different items out with the magazine and ball and send him after the ball again. When he is doing well, start all over again with one of his other toys. When he will get this toy, put it and the ball out together and send him after one toy or the other. Don't correct him if he makes a mistake, just take the toy away from him and try it again. Remember, he's learning a foreign language (yours) and

These two Doxies look like they've been playing too many games and are ready for bed!

at the same time he's trying to figure out what the game is, so be patient.

FIND IT!

When your dog can identify a few items by name, you can hide those items and have him search for them. For example, once he knows the word "keys" you can drop your keys on the floor under an end table next to the sofa. Tell your Dachshund, "Find my keys!" and help him look. Ask "Where are they?" as you move him toward the end table. When he finds them, praise him enthusiastically. Dachshunds use their noses instinctively and are very good at it, so this game should be easy.

As he gets better, make the game more challenging. Make him search in more than one room. Have the item hiding in plain sight or underneath something else. In the beginning, help him, especially when he appears confused. But don't let him give up; make sure he succeeds.

HIDE-AND-SEEK

This is also an easy game for a Dachshund because it encourages him to use his scenting abilities. Begin by having a family member pet your Dachshund, offer him a treat, and then walk away into another room. Tell your Dachshund, "Find Dad!" and let him go. If he runs right to Dad, praise him. Have everyone in the family play the game so that he can learn to search for each one by name.

As he gets better at the game and learns each person's name, the family member hiding will no longer have to pet the dog at the beginning of the game; he can simply go hide. Help your dog initially so that he can succeed at the game, but also encourage him to use his nose and his scenting abilities.

SHAKE HANDS

Shaking hands is a very easy trick to teach. Have your dog sit in front of you. Reach behind one front paw and as you say, "Shake!" tickle his leg in the hollow just behind his paw. When he lifts his paw, shake it gently and praise him. When he starts lifting his paw on his own, stop tickling.

WAVE

When your dog is shaking hands reliably, tell him "Shake. Wave!" and instead of shaking his paw, reach toward it without taking it. Let him touch his paw to your hand, but pull your hand away so that he's

HAVE FUN WITH TRICKS

I taught one of my dogs to play dead and we both had a lot of fun with it. Michi got so good at it that he could pick the phrase "dead dog" out of casual conversation. One day Michi and I had gone to visit the son of a neighbor of mine who had just graduated from the police academy and was very proud of his new uniform. As I shook the police officer's hand to congratulate him, I turned to Michi and asked him, "Would you rather be a cop or a dead dog?" Michi dropped to the ground, went flat on his side, and closed his eyes. The only thing giving him away—that it was all in fun—was the wagging tail. Meanwhile, my neighbor's son was stuttering and turning red. He didn't know whether to be offended or to laugh. It was great fun!

waving. Praise him. Eventually you want him to lift his paw higher than he did for the shake and to move it up and down so he looks like he's waving. You can accomplish that with the movements of your hand as he reaches for it. Praise him enthusiastically when he does it right. When he understands the wave, you can stop using the hand movements.

ROLL OVER

With your Dachshund lying down, take a treat and make a

MAKE UP YOUR OWN TRICKS

What would you and your Dachshund have fun doing? Teach him to stand up on his back legs and dance. Teach him to jump through a hula hoop or through your arms as they form a circle. Teach him to play dead or to sneeze. Trick training is limited only by your imagination and your ability to teach your dog.

circle with your hand around his nose as you tell him, "Roll over." Move the treat in the circular motion to lead his head in the direction you want him to roll. Your other hand may have to help him. Dachshunds have a big rib cage and it may take some effort on your dog's part to start the roll over movement.

Photo by Robert Pearcy

No matter if you are teaching your Doxie to jump through a hoop or just hanging out, spending quality time with your dog is essential in his overall health and well-being.

With a little patience and time, you can achieve great things with your Dachshund.

Photo by Isabelle Francais